'This exciting book gets right to the heart of the i
curriculum. The logic of an aims-based curriculum
the challenge to curriculum designers is set out for
required reading for any teacher about to review
government about to review a national curriculum.....'

Dr Brian Male, Director, The Curriculum Foundation

'... Michael Reiss and John White tackle the most important, but surprisingly the
most neglected, question about the curriculum: not "what should we teach?" but
"why should we teach?". What are the aims of education, what are we trying to
achieve and how should we set about it? Their answers are imaginative and at
the same time grounded in a deep understanding of both the philosophy and the
practice of education: anyone interested in where education is going in the 21st
Century should read this thought-provoking book.'

**Anthony Tomei, Visiting Professor, King's College London, former Director of the
Nuffield Foundation**

'This book is a very welcome challenge to the radical changes which are currently
being imposed upon schools. Starting with a detailed account of the meaning
and aims of education, it continues logically and impressively to demonstrate the
implications for all young people, whatever their abilities and background.'

Professor Richard Pring, Green Templeton College, University of Oxford

An Aims-based Curriculum

IOEPress

The Bedford Way Papers Series

A full list of Bedford Way Papers, including earlier books in the series, can be requested by emailing ioepress@ioe.ac.uk

An Aims-based Curriculum

The significance of human flourishing for schools

Michael J. Reiss and John White

Institute of Education Press
Bedford Way Papers

First published in 2013 by the Institute of Education Press, University of London,
20 Bedford Way, London WC1H 0AL
www.ioe.ac.uk/ioepress

British Library Cataloguing in Publication Data:
A catalogue record for this publication is available from the British Library

ISBN 978 0 85473 998 1

The opinions expressed in this publication are those of the authors and do not necessarily
reflect the views of the Institute of Education, University of London.

Typeset by Quadrant Infotech (India) Pvt Ltd
Printed by CPI Group (UK) Ltd, Croydon, CR0 4YY

Contents

Part 2: Aims into practice 37

About the authors

Michael Reiss is Pro-Director: Research and Development and Professor of Science Education at the Institute of Education, University of London, Chief Executive of Science Learning Centre London, Honorary Visiting Professor at the Universities of Birmingham and York and the Royal Veterinary College, Honorary Fellow of the British Science Association and of the College of Teachers, Docent at the University of Helsinki, Director of the Salters-Nuffield Advanced Biology Project, and an Academician of the Academy of Social Sciences. His books include: Jones, A., McKim, A. and Reiss, M. (eds) (2010) *Ethics in the Science and Technology Classroom: A new approach to teaching and learning*, Sense; Jones, L. and Reiss, M.J. (eds) (2007) *Teaching about Scientific Origins: Taking account of creationism*, Peter Lang; Braund, M. and Reiss, M.J. (eds) (2004) *Learning Science Outside the Classroom*, RoutledgeFalmer; Halstead, J.M. and Reiss, M.J. (2003) *Values in Sex Education: From principles to practice*, RoutledgeFalmer; and Reiss, M.J. (2000) *Understanding Science Lessons: Five years of science teaching*, Open University Press. For further information, see www.reiss.tc

John White is Emeritus Professor of Philosophy of Education at the Institute of Education, University of London, where he has worked since 1965, before which he taught in secondary schools and colleges in Britain and France. His interests are in the mind of the learner and in interrelationships among educational aims and applications to school curricula. Recent books include: *Education and the End of Work* (1997); *Do Howard Gardner's Multiple Intelligences Add Up?* (1998); *Will the New National Curriculum Live Up to its Aims?* (with Steve Bramall) (2000); *The Child's Mind* (2002); *Rethinking the School Curriculum* (ed.) (2004); *The Curriculum and the Child* (2005); *Intelligence, Destiny and Education: The ideological origins of intelligence testing* (2006); *What Schools are For and Why* (2007); *Exploring Well-being in Schools* (2011); and *The Invention of the Secondary Curriculum* (2011).

Introduction

What are schools for? In very general terms, their aims are the same as those of a home with children. The task of both institutions is twofold and simplicity itself, to equip each child:

1. to lead a life that is personally flourishing
2. to help others to do so too.

What schools should do and what homes should do overlap in very many places, and it is a mistake to erect too clear a wall between them. At the same time, schools need a clear picture of what they in particular can best do, and it is the object of this book to provide this. If it is also helpful to parents in showing how what they can do meshes with what schools can do, then so much the better.

The twofold aim may seem too bland and general to guide a country's schools, but it is not. For the general unfolds into the specific, and what may seem empty will prove substantial. From this simply stated aim, all that a country ever needs in a school curriculum can be derived. It generates lesser aims of increasing specificity. Once the framework is in place at the centre, the remaining task of curriculum construction passes to the schools. It is they who fill out the general, nationwide scheme with activities suited to their students and their circumstances.

The approach is very different from how a national curriculum is often planned. Successive ones for England and Wales are typical. They do not begin with overarching aims, then fill them out in greater specificity. Instead, they take for granted a dozen or so discrete school subjects. It is *their* requirements that get filled out.

This has a number of consequences. A subject-led curriculum, especially at secondary level, starts with, and so is necessarily constrained by, the availability of teachers capable of teaching certain subjects. An aims-led curriculum of the sort we argue for here starts with the needs and wants of students. When the National Curriculum for England and Wales was first created in 1988, it had next to no aims to guide it. More recent versions have, it is true, included lists of overall aims, but these have been tacked on to a structure already in place. Crucially, they do not *generate* that structure.

The situation in England and Wales mirrors that in many other parts of the world. A subject-based, rather than an aims-based, curriculum is a global phenomenon. This book argues for a radical change in the way we think of school education. Although we have written it primarily to urge a new policy direction in our own country, the approach it recommends is applicable to any school system.

The major part of the book, Part 1, shows in developing detail how an aims-based curriculum operates. It begins from the twofold aim above, and shows how more specific aims can be derived from this. Section A maps out the larger contours, outlining the major sub-aims to do with the student's own well-being, and the well-being of other people. The far longer Section B goes into further detail about these sub-aims and the more determinate aims to which they point. This section is the core of the book. It enables policy-makers to make the difficult step from very general aims to more specific curriculum content.

Further help on this is provided at the beginning of Part 2, which is all about implementation. As well as giving illustrations of how the aims-structure in Part 1 can be realized in curriculum activities often close to those found in most schools today, it suggests how an aims-based curriculum can be administered at a national level and also within a school. It concludes with a checklist of specific things that a hard-nosed politician should seek to do, so as to move pragmatically from where we are now towards a more fully aims-based system.

As just stated above, Part 1 Section A begins the process of filling out the twofold aim, and Part 1 Section B goes further down this path. Before leaving this Introduction, however, a word about the twofold aim itself.

We hope that it is uncontroversial enough to be taken as a starting point. If we make the very minimal assumption that education – at home and at school – should help people to live flourishing lives, there is every reason in a liberal democratic society why the student's own flourishing should figure largely in this. Other kinds of society may put the weight on the well-being of others to the possible neglect of each individual student. An autocracy or oligarchy may want children to be brought up to serve the interests of the few in power; a utilitarian utopia, to work for the good of all; a theocracy, to carry out what is discerned as God's will. In a democracy, individuals are intrinsically important and their interests are not to be sacrificed to others'.

But individuals also live in a community or, more accurately, in various overlapping communities, and must be educated for this too. If democracies prize everyone's intrinsic well-being, each child should also be brought up to help protect and promote this.

There is still the question of how the two parts of the twofold aim should be related to each other, of where the weight should fall. We come back to this in Part 1 Section A, after unfolding in somewhat more detail what this educational aim involves.

Part

Deriving the aims

1

We have suggested that, in the broadest possible terms, school education should equip every child:

1. to lead a life that is personally flourishing
2. to help others to do so too.

In Section A we shall be fleshing out these aims in somewhat more detail. In the longer Section B we shall take the process of derivation one stage further and will come up with an extensive range of more specific sub-aims.

A first mapping

Here we take each part of the twofold aim separately at first and show in somewhat more detail what it involves. We then show that the two aims are not as separate as they may seem at first sight. We conclude by looking at the broad background knowledge of the world that the twofold aim requires.

Equipping every child to lead a personally flourishing life

There are three components of this aim.

The flourishing life itself

There are many accounts of the flourishing life. Some religious people locate it principally in the afterlife, but this book confines itself to this-world well-being. (At the same time, for those who believe in the existence of an afterlife, there is generally presumed to be a connect between the sort of person we become in this life and who we are in the world to come, so that the argument for an aims-led curriculum is at least as strong.) A hedonist may see it in terms of maximizing pleasurable feelings and minimizing painful ones. More everyday perspectives may tie it to wealth, fame, consumption or, more generally, satisfying one's major desires, whatever these may be. There are difficulties with all these accounts (White 2011a: chs 5–8). A problem besetting the last, and most all-encompassing, of those just mentioned – desire satisfaction – is that it allows ways of life that virtually all of us would deny were flourishing, a life wholly devoted to playing fruit machines, for instance. It also faces the objection that satisfying a major desire – a once-in-a-lifetime holiday, a lottery win, a relationship – can sometimes be bitterly disappointing and so is a poor candidate for fulfilment.

A life filled with wholehearted and successful involvement in more worthwhile pursuits – such things as intimate relationships, meaningful work, making music, scholarly research, gardening, eating good food, watching an excellent film – is on a different plane. Virtually all of us would rate it fulfilling. Some people, not least when writing about education, confine intrinsically worthwhile pursuits to intellectual and aesthetic ones, but the present account is much broader.

Nearly all of us in a modern society like our own assume it is ideally up to us largely to choose the mix of relationships and activities that best suits us (family obligations are generally excepted from this generalization, though less than in the past). This is a central feature of liberal democracy at a time of late modernity (Giddens 1991). Unlike many of our ancestors, nearly all of us are deeply attached to personal autonomy as a value.

A central aim of the school should be to prepare students for a life of autonomous, wholehearted and successful engagement in worthwhile relationships, activities, and experiences (White 2011a: 129–31). With many of these – cooperative work activity, friendships, and enjoying literature for instance – it makes good sense to see that students gain first-hand experience. For others – things like mountaineering, composing symphonies, choosing to live an unmarried life, running a multinational company – *imagined* rather than direct involvement is likely to be more appropriate.

This aim also involves acquainting students with a wide range of possible options from which to choose. With their development towards autonomous adulthood in mind, schools should provide students with increasing opportunities to choose among the pursuits that best suit them. Young children are likely to need greater guidance from their teachers, just as they do from their parents. Part of the function of schooling, and indeed parenting, is to prepare children for the time when they will need to, and will be able to, make decisions more independently. In school, whether curriculum activities are chosen by students or presented to them without choice, the intention should be that students wholeheartedly and enjoyably immerse themselves in them.

Basic needs

If we are to lead a flourishing life, basic needs have to be met. We all need air, water, food, shelter, a certain level of health, a certain level of income. Psychologically, we need companionship, respect, recognition, security and freedom from attack, and freedom from arbitrary arrest and from other impositions (White 2011a: 27–32).

Schools have no hand in meeting some of these needs, like income or a police force. But, in collaboration with parents, they *do* have a contribution to make in encouraging young people to live healthily, for instance, to be sensible in managing money and to value such needs as companionship and freedom from unjustifiable constraints. Schools can also help students to understand their basic needs, the importance of these in their lives, and ways in which they can be met.[1]

Personal qualities

As just implied, there are inward as well as outward necessities: the personal qualities we need if our life is to go well. These include:

- proper regulation of our emotions and our bodily desires for such things as food, drink, sex, and novelty
- a measure of confidence and self-esteem
- independence of thought about the conduct of our life
- determination in carrying through our projects
- good judgement in weighing up conflicting considerations
- fortitude in coping with reverses
- courage, especially moral courage, in the face of fears and anxieties

- appropriate judgements about when we should trust and mistrust others
- sensible attitudes towards risk
- keeping our values in proper perspective, so that we pay due regard to those that are of more, and of less, importance to us.

With these and other dispositions we can all go astray by undershooting or overshooting the mark. Children must learn, for instance, to eat and drink the right sorts of things in roughly the right amounts; to be reasonably independent in their practical judgements, i.e. not overly influenced by peer-group and other pressures, yet willing to listen to and take others' advice where appropriate; not to be overconfident or unduly diffident – and so on through the list. There is every reason why schools should complement the work that good parenting does in this area.

Equipping every child to help others to lead a personally fulfilling life

This aim covers moral education in general, of which one aspect is education for citizenship. Included in the latter is education for work.

Moral education

There is broad agreement about what moral education means. We want children to want other people, as well as themselves, to lead fulfilling lives. Negatively, this means not hurting them, not lying to them, not breaking one's word or in other ways impeding them in this. Positively, it means helping them to reach their goals, respecting their autonomy and being fair, friendly, and cooperative in one's dealings with them.

As with the personal qualities mentioned earlier, schools can reinforce and extend what parents and others in families do in developing morality in children. Schools can widen students' moral sensitivity beyond the domestic circle to those in other communities, locally, nationally and globally. They can also help them to think about moral conflicts in their own lives and in the wider spheres just mentioned. They can encourage students to reflect on the basis of morality, including whether this is religious or non-religious.

Education for citizenship

As part of their moral education, schools should help students to become informed and active citizens of a liberal democratic society. Dispositionally, this means encouraging them to take an interest in political affairs at local, national, and global levels from the standpoint of a concern for the general good; and to do this with due regard to framework values of liberal democracy, such as freedom, individual autonomy, equal consideration, and cooperation. Young people also need to possess whatever sorts of understanding these dispositions entail, for example an understanding of the nature of liberal democracy in general, of divergences of opinion about it, and of its application to the circumstances of their own society.

Education for work

This has to do with equipping students, as future citizens, to contribute to the general well-being, as well as to their own well-being, through work. This will often be remunerated, though much of it (e.g. caring for children or elderly relatives) may not be. As autonomous beings, students will eventually have to make choices about what kind of work to engage in. Schools should be helping them in this, by making them aware of a wide range of vocational possibilities and routes into them, as well as their advantages and disadvantages.

Links between the aims

Although, for convenience of exposition, we have separated one major aim above, to do with the student's own good, from a second, to do with other people's good and covering morality, citizenship, and work, all these aims and sub-aims are interlinked in such a way as to deny their discreteness.

Moral aims are intimately bound up with the civic, including vocational, ones. If moral goodness has to do with making it easier for other people to lead fulfilling lives, one form it takes is helping to maintain and improve the liberal democratic polity necessary for the well-being of all. One aspect of this civic responsibility is helping to provide the goods and services that we all need in order to flourish.

The first aim, to do with the student's own flourishing, is not separable, in turn, from the second, to do with others'. They *would* be discrete, if promoting one person's interests were something self-contained, disconnected from promoting other people's.

But this misrepresents how things are (White 2011a: ch.10). A person's own flourishing revolves around all kinds of valuable relationships and activities. All of these relationships, and very many of the other activities, further other people's well-being as well as one's own. Think of intimate friendships, of teaching or nursing as a career, of other collaborative pursuits of all sorts, even of more isolated activities like painting pictures, given the pleasure that others often get from these.[2]

One of the reasons why the inseparability of personal and moral aims may be hard to see is the error of thinking that for a person to lead a flourishing life, he or she must *aim* to do so. This is not so. In order to flourish, you must want your beloved to be happy, your children to be fed, your garden to be attractive, your patients to get well. But you do not have to have the *further* aim of becoming personally fulfilled through doing such things. Keeping your own interests in your sights may in fact make it *harder* for you to succeed as a lover, parent, teacher, etc., since it divides your attention, turning you away from wholehearted immersion in what is at hand.

The argument to this point underlines the especial importance of personal fulfilment as an educational aim. We saw above how it should not be sacrificed to the good of others. Now we see how closely connected these two things often are. In equipping children for a flourishing life, we are at the same time developing them as moral beings, as workers and as citizens: in all these domains, people can get involved in all kinds of valuable pursuits and therein find fulfilment.

Broad background understanding

There is a further link between the two major aims, important enough to deserve a section of its own. Whatever we do in our lives that brings us personal benefit, or is intended to benefit others, takes place against a broad background of thoughts about the world we live in. Closest to home are thoughts about what sort of beings we are. We all grow up to believe, for instance, that we will live at most for a century or so; that we may or may not stay healthy; that the future has a considerable element of unpredictability. We all come to see our lives as inextricably bound up with the lives of other human beings. These perceptions alone cannot but influence the way we lead our lives.

These thoughts about our human nature are only one part of the background. We see ourselves as living creatures, related in some way or other to other living things. We think of the life around us – animal and vegetable – against the backdrop of the Earth on which it occurs, and Earth itself as part of the solar system and ultimately of the universe.

Every human society must conduct its day-to-day affairs against some kind of background. Our own society's, unlike most in the past, is partly shaped by science. As a result, much of our background consists of presumptions about which there is little or no reasonable doubt: the belief that the Earth goes round the Sun, for instance, rather than vice versa. At a more fundamental level – when we reach the question why there is anything at all – for many of us the background includes other things than presumptions: puzzlement, the sense that we shall never know the answer, speculations about what the answer may be. It is because the background need not consist only of presumptions that we used above the more-encompassing word 'thoughts' to describe it.

Part of the task of education – at home and at school – is to help children to form this background that will colour everything they do. Much of it will consist of well-founded scientific conclusions – about the social nature of human beings, for instance, or about the movement of planets. At a more fundamental level, some of us will live by religious or other beliefs that give us answers to the deep questions, while others will live without such beliefs. While at a less fundamental level there is every reason why children should be inducted into the science that informs it, once we reach ultimate questions the role of education is less clear-cut, though good education has an important role to play in clarifying the boundaries of knowledge. We will be returning to this in the context of giving greater specificity to the most general aims.

Meanwhile, what this section has revealed is that the two general aims with which we began have now led us towards a *third* aim underpinning these two: helping children to form the background just described.

The next step

The next section takes us from the most general aims to lower-level aims derivable from them. The more these lower-level aims are filled in, the closer we get to something with which most of us are familiar: detailed statements of curriculum objectives found in national curriculum handbooks across the world.

But there is a crucial difference. Conventional curriculum objectives are organized within academic disciplines, whose importance to education tends to be taken as read. A good education, so common wisdom goes, is based around mother tongue, mathematics, science, history, geography, art, music, etc. Few start further back, as this book does, and ask what schools are *for*. In this publication, the more familiar curriculum objectives are derived from general aims, *not* from the specialist requirements of particular disciplines.

This is likely to mean, in turn, some *divergence* from conventional curriculum content and objectives. It would be remarkable indeed if this aims-based approach to the curriculum resulted in precisely the same expectations and priorities as the more familiar chain of reasoning. How extensive any divergence is we can only see as the details of the present scheme are filled in. We now turn to this task.

Making the aims more determinate

We move, then, from the general aims to rather more determinate aims into which they unfold. Including the background aim, with which we begin, there are now three general aims of schools:

1. helping every student to form a broad background of understanding
2. equipping every student to lead a personally flourishing life
3. equipping every student to help others to lead personally flourishing lives.

Broad background understanding

Students need to be helped to understand their own nature and that of other people as human beings. This has a biological aspect: they need to understand something of how they function biologically, and also how they are connected with the rest of the animal, and wider living, world.

Some grasp of evolutionary theory, genetics, and child development is essential here. But there is also a cultural aspect: human beings, as language users, are the only animals (setting aside the beginnings of self-consciousness seen in a few other species) known to be conscious of their own existence. Students need to be inducted into the implications of this for our social life, including its forms of cooperation and its intellectual and artistic achievements.

Part of this self- and other-understanding is about not being imprisoned within contested beliefs about human beings that may hinder one's own and others' flourishing. These may include the belief that we all have individually differing limits of intellectual ability, as well as myths – often related to this – about class-based, religious, gender-related, national or ethnic superiority and inferiority.

Students should also know something about the main features of human prehistory and history, from earliest human life through the coming of agriculture and city life to the invention of printing, the rise of global trade, the arrival of industrialization and mechanization, and our own increasingly knowledge-based age.

Evolutionary perspectives are also central to students' understanding of the living world of animal and plant life within its varying geographical and geological contexts.

Their background will also include elementary astronomical knowledge of the place of the Earth and other planets in our solar system, and of the relation of that system to the wider universe. It will also take them into what is known about how the universe operates, its fundamental constituents at molecular, atomic, and sub-atomic levels, its chemical composition and the basic forces that direct it.

This aim also engages learners with ultimate questions about why there is anything at all, about how and why the universe came into being, and about the relationship between consciousness, including self-awareness, and the material world. They should be acquainted with religious and non-religious perspectives on these issues and encouraged to assess them and to reach their own autonomous conclusions about them.

Although this aim embraces the transmission of much knowledge, not least scientific knowledge, this is always in the service of helping children to build up a background. Indeed, there has been a move within science education in favour of such a 'cultural' argument for school science. In other words, one function of science education is seen as enabling students better to appreciate the contribution of science to our cultural milieu, or 'background' as we put it here. Big ideas are more important in this than specifics, and accumulating knowledge is in the interests of reflection on, and discussion about, the bigger picture that is being put together (Harlen 2010). Other aspects of science come up later under different headings and include more specific requirements.

Because a background of this sort has an indispensable role in a worthwhile human life, curriculum activities surrounding it must be compulsory for all students, though this leaves open whether such compulsion is for the whole of the duration of schooling or not.

Equipment for personal flourishing

We take in turn the three components of this aim:

1. the flourishing life itself
2. basic needs
3. personal qualities.

The flourishing life itself

This aim is about preparing students for wholehearted and successful involvement in valuable activities and relationships. Given the interconnections between all the aims, these activities and relationships include many of moral, vocational, and civic significance. We start with relationships.

RELATIONSHIPS

These cover a wide range: intimate relationships among family members, friends and eventually, for most of us, lovers; collegiate relationships with those with whom one works, at school and in later life; thinner relationships with strangers, again at different levels – face-to-face, within local communities, fellow citizens of one's country, people in other countries, people as yet unborn. These relationships can enrich one's personal life, making it more fulfilling.

Good intimate relationships are, for virtually all of us, pivotal to our well-being. They have not always been high on schools' agendas. School friendships have sometimes even been considered as threats to learning. These days, schools are more likely to see them as intrinsically important and worthy of fostering. That having been said, schools in virtually all countries are generally very conservative in any sex and relationships education they provide. They typically focus on a narrow reproductive view of sex and sexuality, or stress 'problems' about sexual behaviour. We are not so naive or starry-eyed to believe that sexual relationships are never problematic but, for most of us, they can also be places where we receive, and give, great pleasure and they play an important role in human flourishing. Schools could do more to enable students to reflect on their sexual hopes (Halstead and Reiss 2003).

What schools can or should do *directly* to facilitate friendships and other intimate relationships is obviously limited. This is patently so in the area of sexual intimacy, but also on a wider front. But there are immense opportunities for *imaginative* involvement in close relationships via the arts, especially fiction, film, drama, and poetry.

Friendship merges with relationships with others who are working with one on a common task. Here the school can have a more direct role. It can and should encourage cooperative activities, for example classroom projects and discussions, team games, out-of-school activities. These can contribute in themselves to students' flourishing, as well as preparing them in later life to become good colleagues and collaborators at work and outside it.

We will not go through more distant relationships in detail, but focus on one aspect of them by way of example: relationships with people in other countries. The interconnectedness of people's lives and fates across the globe is now increasingly appreciated. Children need gradually to come to see this in its many aspects. They need some understanding of our economic and ecological interdependence, of poorer and richer areas, of moral issues about aid and justice. Stereotypes of all sorts can get in the way of fruitful relationships across countries and these, too, should be discussed and understood. Links based on religion, a common language, and shared interests are another focus, as is technological progress via the internet and in other ways to bring people from different countries closer together.

Students should be brought up to value these global relationships and to see them as part of their own well-being. If we put all the emphasis on *actual* relationships, it may well seem that the school's role has to be limited to such things as links with overseas schools, encouraging internet pen-friendships, and the like. But once we add to this what can be accomplished by the imagination working on our emotions, possibilities become endless. Fiction of a non-stereotyping sort in film and print, as well as documentary material, can help students to feel what it is (or was) like to be a person living in a totalitarian regime, a black person in the deep South of the USA, or an Indian peasant migrating to the city. Fictional portrayals of family life, love affairs, and other close relationships set in other parts of the world likewise engage students' emotions.

All this helps them to see, not only in an intellectual way but also at the level of sympathetic involvement, that human beings, for all their differences in culture and circumstances, have fundamental similarities in their needs, aspirations, and relationships.

ACTIVITIES

We also flourish when fully and successfully engaged in intrinsically worthwhile activities of all sorts. Relationships come into these, too, and substantially. Friends make music together; work activities are generally collaborative. But we focus now on worthwhile activities themselves.

There is a huge range of these. Their very extensiveness creates a problem for the curriculum planner. They cover all kinds of creative and spectatorial aesthetic pursuits, built around love of nature as well as love of art; meaningful work of all kinds (seeing that this can be intrinsically fulfilling, as well as having a valuable end-product); other practical interests, from cookery to pigeon racing; the pursuit of knowledge and understanding for its own sake; physical exercise; travel; helping other people ... How can all this and more be reflected in the school curriculum?

A basis for choice

In a liberal democracy we expect people, as autonomous beings, to make their own choices about the activities that most suit them. One role of the school is to prepare children to make these choices – not on a once-for-all-time basis, of course, but throughout their lives.

Part of this preparation is being acquainted with a wide range of intrinsically valuable activities as a basis for choice. It would not be sensible for curriculum-makers to aim at comprehensiveness at a detailed level. There are simply so many different kinds of sport, of meaningful work, and of other practical activities that this would not be feasible. In any case, why comprehensiveness? None of us needs to be acquainted with *every* activity in order to make autonomous choices and enjoy their fruits. Many, indeed, lead very full lives with far less baggage.

If we were to try to give children *first-hand involvement* in every detailed kind of activity, our task would be even more daunting. It might well take a lifetime. Fortunately, there is a short cut, if not to comprehensiveness, to acquaintance with many areas of activity. You don't have actually to ski to know *something* about what it would be like to ski. This may not be enough for you to be sure that skiing either is or is not for you, and perhaps nothing could clinch this short of actual experience. Until one has tried skiing – or making a pot or remaining silent for 48 hours – one has only a partial appreciation of what such activities entail. But an outsider's knowledge about the activity can take you some part of the way. What takes you even further is *imagined involvement* gained from book, Wii, or film material about skiing. We have already mentioned this role of the imagination when talking about relationships. It has immense potential in the activities area, too. Think of what we can learn from art and documentary works about what it would be like to work as an engineer, a barrister, a front-line soldier, a midwife, or to go in for country pursuits, foreign travel, writing novels, politics ...

To some extent, then, students can acquire their 'basis for choice' from sources other than first-hand involvement. In other cases, first-hand involvement is preferable.

This is one thing to bear in mind when seeing how the activities' aims are to issue in more determinate curricular objectives. Another is how far a 'basis for choice' points to curricular pursuits that should be compulsory for every student, as distinct from optional. We come back to this below.

It may be tempting to try to work out definitively which activities need first-hand involvement and which do not. Work in that general direction may be necessary at some point, but unless we are very careful, we may find ourselves getting into complex curriculum taxonomies, which prevent us from seeing the wood for the trees.[3] At this point in this book, we do not need further complexity, but a reminder of what we are centrally about.

Wholehearted involvement: in life and in school

The aspect of school education with which we are currently dealing is enabling learners to lead fulfilling lives – more specifically, lives of wholehearted and successful engagement in all sorts of valuable activities. Wholeheartedness here should not be taken to mean an abandonment of critical faculties. Indeed, it is only by wholeheartedly throwing oneself into competitive team sports, opera and multiplayer video games, for example, that one can validly decide to abandon subsequent engagement with them.

More generally, if part of what schools should be preparing students for is lives of enthusiastic engagement in valuable activities, what better way of doing this than by filling their school day, as far as realistically possible, with activities that they find enjoyable and wholly absorbing, and in which they can find success? This is not always the first thing that curriculum-makers have in mind, but it should have a high priority. It wins out over trying to give students an exhaustive acquaintance with every type of knowledge and every aspect of one's culture.

In large measure, the test is what young people do once their school days are in the past. It is not much good if they have covered all curriculum bases, only to emerge switched off from learning. Much better that they are eager to carry on, even though there are what some would see as gaps in their accomplishments. If students are eager, they have the best part – perhaps 60 or more years – of a lifetime left to fill them.

Personal fulfilment pivots around wholeheartedness of involvement. We all know what this is like from those times in our lives when we are utterly absorbed in what we are doing, when we are not distracted or easily interrupted, when, as some would say, we lose all sense of self or passing time, when things flow.

If this is what we want people regularly to experience throughout their lives, it makes good sense to start young. With *very* young children, this is often very easy. A typical 4-year-old has no problem about this kind of total immersion. Unless things have been going badly in their lives, children of that age do not carry deep anxieties around with them. They are too young to be beset with money worries, gnawing regrets, unrealistic ambitions, insoluble relationship problems. They throw themselves into their gyrations on the monkey bars and dressing up with enviable intenseness. They have nothing to shut out.

As children grow towards maturity, they become more like the rest of us. The cares of the world begin to intrude. Wholeheartedness becomes, for most of us, an ideal that we attain only intermittently – in those stretches of time when we shut out the extraneous and live, as we say, for the moment. Of course, from a well-being perspective, wholeheartedness is not always a plus. Absorption can be into the worthless or harmful – compulsive fruit-machining, screen-watching, binge drinking. Schools are there to encourage its more valuable forms.

Ideally, that is. In practice, having to fit in with curriculum exigencies, even quite young children can lose their early years' raptness. For some, prison-house shades descend before they leave primary school. Diligence alone is no protection. 'Good' students can assimilate everything that the curriculum demands of them, come top in tests, and scoop honours in public examinations, yet grind through their studies in an industrious but unenthused way. Things could be so much better.

Compulsory activities

This is why the foremost priority should be wholehearted engagement. This can come about in compulsory activities or in optional ones. What considerations should we rely on, in deciding which worthwhile activities belong to each category?

We have seen already that, as a basis for choice, there is normally no need to *oblige* children to engage in activities in which imagined (rather than actual) involvement can open up its attractions for them, at least to some extent. Nor is just imagination needed. We can get some idea of what travel to far-off lands might be like from a single visit to somewhere closer to home, yet unfamiliar. A run on a cheap sled can be an intimation of the Vallée Blanche. Educators can leave it to students to pursue such activities if they choose, sometimes – where appropriate – as an optional activity at school. Here, playing the drums can make more sense than playing the organ, weekend youth hostelling more sense than polar exploration.

Where worthwhile activities are less accessible outside school, there may be a stronger case for compulsion within school. So, schools should introduce students to a foreign language and teach them about atheism and religious belief, as too many children won't get these well taught by their families or through other extraschool means. But this is not without qualification. Suppose there is some fiendishly complicated game (i.e. it takes a very long time to derive pleasure from it) that aficionados enjoy but that is virtually impossible to explain to an outsider or even a beginner. There is no good reason that we can see why we should insist that every child get inside it.

This suggests that the compulsory activities now under discussion should at least be beneficial for (virtually) every student's flourishing. This is vague as yet, but examples may help.

- *An illustration: mathematics and literature.* Compare mathematical activity beyond basic numerical skills with reading imaginative literature. If we go by how adults who have studied both at school choose to spend their free time, while many of them are into (non-trashy) novels, drama, or poetry, it seems that few tend to devote their spare evenings to algebra or geometry.[4] Why so?

Good literature is in large measure about human life: relationships, ambitions, imperfections of character, amusing things, successes and failures – things that most of us find endlessly fascinating. Pure mathematics is a universe in itself. Writers, moreover, use all kinds of methods to seduce us further into their texts: suspense, wit, arresting language ... It is not surprising that readers get – willingly – drawn into them and look forward to more experiences of the same sort. For most of us, mathematics is beyond such welcome manipulation.

But this divergence of interest between the two areas is not enough to give literature a greater place in a compulsory curriculum than mathematics. It gestures towards a good argument, but more is needed.

Pulp fiction, soap operas, and B movies are *also* about human life and relationships. Their authors and directors know all about getting an audience hooked. But we rightly do not rate them highly as educational vehicles. Indeed, we sometimes see them as *anti*-educational – if, for instance, they reinforce stereotypes, rather than challenge them.

This is not to say that reading or watching such material can add nothing to the flourishing life. It can be pleasurable and absorbing enough in its place. But all too often it does not take us far into the subtleties of human lives and cultures, nor does it involve us at a reflective as well as an emotional level in deeper insights into our common human nature. Works that do so have far better credentials as educational material.[5]

Literature is important to all of us, partly because of its role in helping us to form a background of understanding. It can not only fill out our appreciation of our shared human nature, including its relation to the rest of nature and the universe, but it also invites us to take pleasure in reflecting about this. This is inseparable from reflectiveness about our own and other people's values, about their priorities, and conflicts between them as our life unfolds. These considerations take us into the territory of the personal qualities that help each of us to live in a fulfilling way. We come back to these personal qualities below.

As an activity pursued for its own sake, reading literature scores well, then, as a contributor to a flourishing life. How well does mathematics do?

For its devotees, it takes you into a self-contained world of great fascination and aesthetic delight. For them, there is no doubt about its importance for their own well-being. But is it important to everyone's? It is hard to make a case for this. Precisely because it *is* self-contained, it does not have literature's power to illuminate aspects of the human condition that we all share.

All this suggests that studying post-basic mathematics for its own sake has far less claim to a place in the compulsory curriculum than studying literature. It points at most to an obligatory 'taster' course, designed to whet learners' appetites for going further if they wish, in an optional course (Bramall and White 2000). Of course there may be *other* reasons – extrinsic rather than intrinsic ones – for some compulsory mathematics beyond the basics; we return to this possibility later.

• *Compulsory, taster and optional courses.* The discussion of mathematics and literature poses a challenge to the conventional way national governments construct school curricula. They take compulsory activities as the norm over the 10 to 12 years of compulsory schooling. They carve teaching hours over this expanse of time into great blocks of time: in England, for instance, 11 years of English, mathematics, science and religious education, 9 years of history, geography, music, and so on.

Switching to an aims-based curriculum yields a more principled, more flexible approach. It favours compulsory activities only where there are good reasons for them. In the argument to date, this applies to activities concerned with the background, and to intrinsic engagement with literature.[6] We come to others as we proceed.

As to how long, or how continuous, compulsory courses should be – whether they are to be 1, 2, or 10 years, and whether there are gaps in them – these questions, too, are still up for discussion. It is best not to decide on them before the whole picture of curriculum priorities has been filled in. Some decisions will in any case fall on schools: these are outside the political realm to which this book is mainly confined.[7]

Not that whatever turns out to be compulsory has to be monolithically so. Literature teachers will want to make sure that students suck the marrow out of their subject, but they can do this and still leave them plenty of choice about what they read and when.

There is every reason why they should do so. Opportunities for choice are essential when building up a child's disposition to live as an autonomous person. They are also likely to facilitate wholeheartedness of involvement.

For many activities pursued for their own sake, the pattern that has emerged in the discussion of post-basic mathematics may well be appropriate: a taster course

– length unspecified – followed by options for those so inclined.[8] Sometimes, options alone may be appropriate. One or other of these patterns may fit such things as gardening, studying architecture, exploring transport systems, or taking further some specialized aspect of science, engineering, literature, or art and design. Since comprehensive coverage is less important than satisfying involvement, schools should have some leeway in the optional activities they provide.

Some activities that are usually compulsory for all ages in actual school curricula may better suit a taster/option model. For example, in so far as healthy physical exercise is an aim of PE classes, this does not require compulsory classes year on year, only time set aside for it and in individual cases some encouragement. After all, some students will obtain enough exercise for physical health outside school. More specialized PE activities, like gym work and various sports, could be built into optional programmes backed by taster activity. So, perhaps, could practical artistic activities like singing, some drawing and painting, playing an instrument, writing poetry. In England, where we speak a globally used language, but not perhaps in Finland, modern foreign languages (MFLs) might also be taught on a taster/option basis. A common justification for compulsory MFLs is that they will be useful in later life, at work or otherwise; other reasons are that they help us to appreciate another culture, and to understand language as a general phenomenon. Experts in the field have cast doubt on the cogency of these claims (Williams 2000, Hawkins 2005). In any case, many of those who warm to MFLs at school do so for *intrinsic* reasons; unlike many of their peers, they just enjoy these kinds of linguistic activities. If so, and in the absence of good reasons for compulsion, this would seem to speak in favour of the taster/option model.

To come back to compulsory activities – those that students are expected to gain more than a taste of as a basis for choice – what, if anything, can we add to background studies (which we argued include a considerable amount of science), basic mathematics and imaginative literature?[9]

It is tempting to think within conventional categories, of further school *subjects* that ought to be obligatory. We shall indeed be looking at some of these, or aspects of them, in a moment. But let us meanwhile think outside that frame about other intrinsically valuable *activities* that all should follow.

Thinking is one such. It takes many forms: the reflection on human nature and our existence in the universe that we discussed in the sections on background; practical reasoning about what we are going to do (in designing things, for instance, in our relationships, in our involvement in wider social concerns, etc.); the contemplation of aesthetic objects; imagining other scenarios; theoretical thinking within an academic discipline … All these, no less than swimming, painting a wall, or walking in the woods are types of *activity*. Like these other things, as well as any extrinsic purpose they may have, they are also capable of being enjoyed for their own sake. Strangely, in their preoccupation with passing on factual knowledge, schools sometimes give this important activity short shrift. There is a strong case for seeing that thinking, in all its forms, is a non-negotiable part of every student's experience throughout his or her school life. A task for every school is to help learners to throw themselves as wholeheartedly into this activity as they would into a favourite sport or hobby.

A lot of thinking is silent and solitary, and schools should make due provision for this. But it can also be vocal and social, as in class discussions. These are an excellent vehicle for thinking as an activity. Sometimes, not least in primary schools, they fall under the rubric of 'philosophy' sessions. These can be impressive in encouraging children to discuss issues in a way that respects others, and at the same time with enjoyment and commitment. The label 'philosophy' may be an impediment, as it draws attention away from the fact that thinking activities can take many shapes – not all, by a far cry, a philosophical one (White 2012).

Group discussion is a cooperative activity, but there are also many other forms of this: working together on a theoretical investigation, like developments in medical care in the last two centuries; or on a practical project, like ways of making the school environment safer; in a musical group; as part of a sports team. Schools can support this on an optional basis, as in the last two examples, but there is a case for building it into a compulsory requirement throughout the school, as in the first two. For the great majority of people, collaborative activity is intrinsically enjoyable as well as useful for some further end, and can foster personal, moral, and civic virtues discussed elsewhere in this book.

To go back to more traditional curriculum activities that should be compulsory, enjoying non-literary arts – paintings, sculpture, architecture, film, music, dance – shares many of the same features as engagement in literature. Experiencing the more subtle and exquisite delights of these areas is helped enormously by induction into them by experts. People introduced to their various forms and genres tend in adult life to prize this kind of activity as part of what makes their life worth living. Like verbal arts – but more tacitly, through sound and sight and touch – these have the power of constantly reconnecting us with background thoughts and feelings about the strangeness and fleetingness of our being in the world. It is because these arts are so central to our flourishing that there should be a substantial place for them on a compulsory basis. This is compatible, of course, with optional classes in the particular arts, within this system.

Aspects of the physical[10] sciences – as well as of the psychological and social sciences – are already within the compulsory area in virtue of their background importance. Other aspects, including applications of science, join them via work-related education (discussed below). Together, they provide a rich area of study that young people can enjoy for its own sake. Again, there can be more specialized optional activities within this.

History as a discrete subject is a staple of the conventional compulsory curriculum (Cannadine *et al.* 2011). Aspects of it are also non-negotiable in the present scheme, but these are derived from wider aims of education. We have seen how background aims necessitate a grasp of the main features of human prehistory and history. We see later how civic aims require some understanding of how our own society and developments across the globe have come to be what they are. As ever, such extrinsic considerations are compatible with a passion for historical enquiry for its own sake, and, as ever, it would be good if schools could encourage further work on specialized areas of enquiry on an optional basis.

CONCLUSION

This long section on the flourishing life has been about the involvement in relationships and in activities that contributes to this. Although we have looked at this area analytically, aspect by aspect, it is crucial to remember that whether or not a person is leading a flourishing life is a question about that life (or a time-slice of it) as a whole. We are talking about the whole mosaic of a person's relationships and activities. It is up to him or her, as an autonomous person, to shape this. This is likely to be a complex matter, involving decisions about priorities, testing things out, backtracking, trying to keep the fragile web of all one's interconnected concerns intact. We say more about this in the section below on the personal qualities needed for the flourishing life (see page 25).

We are aware, too, that the discussion of intrinsically valuable activities in this section, lengthy though it is, could be expanded yet further. This reflects the difficulty, perhaps the impossibility, of marshalling all the relevant items within a tidy scheme. This difficulty casts doubt on attempts that some curriculum-makers have traditionally made in this area to produce timetable-friendly schemes based on classifications at once demarcated and complete. The untidiness, such as it is, need not be as troublesome as it may seem. Schools can remind themselves that they are not in the business of covering the ground, either here or elsewhere. Their task is to lay foundations, or, changing the metaphor, to open up vistas. There is no set way of doing this. What is required in this, as in every area we discuss, is intelligent, flexible thinking that keeps educational aims always in view. We give one or two on-the-ground examples of this in Part 2 (see 'Aims-based planning within the school', page 52).

Basic needs

We need to fill out the brief account of education in this area given earlier (see page 6). As we saw, some basic needs – income, for instance – are not the school's responsibility to provide, while it does have some role in other cases – encouraging students to live healthily, for instance.

DISPOSITIONS

The second of these categories, i.e. basic needs that are part of the school's role to provide, includes not only health but also sensible money management. In both these areas, schools can help to build up desirable dispositions.

In health education, they can encourage students to eat and drink sensibly, to take exercise, to be wary of irreversibly damaging limbs, organs, or other parts of the body. They can also help to protect and improve mental health – by working with children to make them less anxious, for instance. On health, as elsewhere, they can work with parents to build up desirable habits. We will come back to this below (see page 24).

In the area of money management, schools can reinforce positive attitudes towards sensible behaviour, avoiding extremes of profligacy on the one hand and miserliness or niggardliness on the other. There is a place here for group discussion, projects involving imaginary situations, as well as lessons from fiction and drama. We will come back to our basic need for an adequate income when we look at work aims below (see page 32).

Another basic need is recognition. We all want others around us to think well of us; we thrive when they warm to us as people or think well of our achievements, languish when they disdain or, sometimes worse, ignore us. Schools can support a regime of mutual recognition-giving, among students and staff alike. Part of their task is to help children to keep the desire for recognition within sensible bounds, not making it too prominent in their value systems so that they crave it at every end and turn. Making students aware of social and commercial pressures towards status-seeking and becoming a celebrity (including famous for being famous) falls under this end.

Closely associated with recognition is companionship. Few of us flourish as isolated individuals; we need to be bonded with others around us in various degrees of closeness. In the past, this may not have been considered within the school's province, but if we are now turning towards an aims-based programme of the sort envisaged, rather than leaving students to cope with the demands of a traditional curriculum, we have to be more attentive to their social needs and should no longer treat them as isolated learners.

Freedom from constraints, except where these are necessary to prevent harm to others, is not a basic human need if we are thinking merely of survival, but for nearly everyone it is a condition of flourishing as an autonomous person in a liberal democracy. Schools can do much to accustom students to taking freedom as a necessary background feature of their lives. Since schools, especially primary schools, are dealing with immature people, much of what they do has to be within a compulsory framework. However, there is every reason to build unconstrained elements into this, as well as encouraging optional activities and free time within and after the school day. Schools are also in an excellent position to encourage older learners to discuss and reflect on the significance of freedom in relation to autonomy, well-being, and a liberal democratic society.

Finally, we should perhaps state that education itself is a basic need. Given the sort of creatures human beings are, we need a lengthy induction into desirable ways of behaving and thinking, as well as the kinds of understanding that these require. These requirements can be met through home schooling, supplemented by activities that take place away from the home without schooling. Nevertheless, for all that it is growing in popularity in a number of countries, this is likely to remain a minority way of providing for children's education.

These are some examples, but not an exhaustive list, of basic needs that schools can directly help to meet, partly in collaboration with families. In each case, a particular emphasis so far has been on fostering appropriate dispositions and attitudes.

UNDERSTANDING

An adequate income, somewhere to live, and security on the streets as well as from foreign attack are also necessary conditions of personal well-being. Schools have no direct role in helping to satisfy their students' needs of this sort, but that does not mean they have nothing to do here.

For all basic needs, the ones just mentioned as well as those discussed in the last section, schools can help students to understand what these are and why they are important to our flourishing. '*Our* flourishing' includes both each student's own well-being and that of other people. Part of the moral work of the school (see 'Moral education' below) is reinforcing the point that it should *matter* to children that others in their local community and elsewhere in the world have adequate health provision, education, income, shelter, freedom from interference, and the rest.

The demands on students' understanding are many, and many-sided. In health education, they include aspects of science; in money management and the provision of housing, they include health, education, and a police force, and some grasp of economics, politics, and social science; in recognition and mental health, they include an acquaintance with psychology; and in issues to do with the place of basic needs in a person's well-being, they include thinking and discussion of a philosophical sort. We will be picking up related points about demands on understanding in later sections.

Personal qualities

Schools can work with parents in reinforcing the personal qualities that each of us needs to lead a flourishing life. We first discussed these on page 6 and came across some of them again – those connected with our basic health and financial needs – on page 22.

We all have innate physical desires for food, drink, sexual activity, and exercise, and must learn to manage these in our own interests, as well as those of other people. In each case there is no simple formula. We have to learn through experience and thought what are the sensible things to do in different circumstances. With eating and drinking, for instance, it makes sense, health-wise, to keep one's energy intake within certain bounds, to eat plenty of fruit and vegetables, and not to drink alcohol to excess. But occasional party times license more indulgence. We also have to learn to eat and drink in appropriate ways – sometimes sitting up to table but sometimes having to snatch a sandwich on the go. It is good to bring children up not with rigid rules, but through intelligent education to do what is fitting on different occasions.

In our commercial culture, dispositions of this sort have to be shored up by those of another sort. Since there is constant pressure on children to eat and drink too much, and too much of the wrong things, they need to be steeled against these blandishments – again, not in an over-rigid way so that they always mistrust advertisements, but in a more discerning manner. This is an argument for the inclusion of media studies in the curriculum, whether as a subject in its own right or embedded within other subjects.

Sexual desire and performance are also prey to commercial manipulation. Here again, schools and parents need to work in complementary fashion to help young people intelligently to manage this sensitive area. It can be difficult for students to admit sexual ignorance, while schools can too easily find themselves providing a message that sexual activity is only about risks and problems (sexually transmitted infections, unwanted pregnancies).

We are all creatures not only of bodily desirings but also of emotions. The theme of learning to feel, think, and do the right things at the right times, in the right circumstances, and in the right ways applies here, too. Managing one's fears and anxieties is part of learning to become a courageous person. For most of us, this has less to do with intrepidity in playground fights or on other battlefields than with sensible, flexible reactions to different sorts and manifestations of harm, real or imagined – road traffic, the dark, infections, spiders, bullies, speaking in public. Educators also have a role in encouraging students to be able to stand out against inappropriate peer-group pressure where their own and others' interests are concerned. We have focused on the management of fear, but similar points could and should be made about other emotions that impact on one's own well-being and the well-being of others, like anger, joy, self-love, resentment, shame, and guilt.

We come next to dispositions that help students to manage their lives more generally. It is questionable whether they need education in large-scale life-planning. Sometimes the desirability of this gets taken as read. Older students are often urged to map out their lives ahead, especially as regards a career. Families and schools sometimes feel they can breathe again when they know that Carrie is now set on becoming an orthodontist and has an excellent idea of the exam results she needs for this. There is an issue here of whether life-planning is a *sine qua non* of a flourishing life. Some people seem to thrive with a laid-back attitude, responding more spontaneously to whatever comes their way. Is suggesting to young people that they should be charting out their lives years ahead a kind of paternalism?

Long-term planning apart, sensible smaller-scale management of our lives is vital to our well-being. As we grow, we need to develop practical rationality. This is many-sided. It involves some clarity about our goals – not life-goals necessarily, but those found in shorter-term and everyday projects. It requires flexibility in adapting means to ends in pursuit of our goals, as well as sensitivity to which means are acceptable from a moral point of view. Good on-the-spot judgement is also necessary: unforeseen events can crop up in any venture, and we have to learn to react to them appropriately. These include obstacles that must be overcome if the original aim is not to be abandoned, and may also involve clashes between values – clashes that require immediate resolution (as when a young person or any of us is just off to a party, and a friend calls round in some distress and wants to talk things through). Practical rationality also entails dispositions like perseverance, not being daunted by setbacks, and not being easily sidetracked or tempted into other paths, by peer-group pressure or other things.

Practical rationality manifests itself, too, in more reflective dispositions, less tied to activity of the moment. Clashes of value crop up not only in immediate events, as in the example given. They are endemic in our lives as a whole. Should I continue with my plan to become a lawyer, or would I do better to trust to my talent for painting? Is security more important to me than risk? Do I think too much of my own interests, when I could be doing so much to help reduce poverty in the world? Personal flourishing demands some ability to keep our values in some kind of order, including a hierarchy of what is more and what is less important to us. And since this order is not fixed throughout our lives, we have to get into the habit of revisiting our value scheme from time to time.

The distinction between the personal qualities needed for courses of action and the more reflective virtues just mentioned itself gives rise to another conflict of values that each of us has to learn to resolve. Just how reflective should I be? As the kind of person who likes getting on with things, why shouldn't I just do this? Can't I leave philosophizing to those inclined that way? Or am I in danger of living in a blinkered way? But if I get too wrapped up in thought, mightn't I become a Hamlet figure, endlessly debating with myself, never taking action?

These are some of the personal qualities that students need to develop for a fulfilling personal life. They need other dispositions, too – ones that bear on their moral relationships with others, and we will be coming to these below (see page 26). Some may say that parents alone are responsible for fostering personal qualities, and schools should restrict themselves to academic tasks. But acquiring dispositions is an ongoing and ever-deepening process. Schools, as custodians of their students for around six or seven hours a day, should be reinforcing patterns that good parents have already laid down. They can organize their curriculum activities and other features of school life partly with this in mind. It is easy to see how school policies on meals, break times, pedagogy, health education, sex and relationships education, discipline, and personal counselling can support this. Extended projects can be well suited to promote the executive virtues like goal-setting, working out means to ends, on-the-spot judgement, pertinacity, coping with setbacks, and so on. Literature and drama lend themselves to work on the reflective virtues, as well as, more generally, reminding readers and spectators of the place of *all* the dispositions touched on in this section in a human life. These goals are also well served by that most neglected learning activity in an age of fact-processing and reproducing – discussion.

We have already stressed the value of imagining things. Imagination can help us to envisage how our lives might be different now or develop in the future. Equally, imagination can help us to understand others better, increasing empathy and leading us to be less judgemental.

Somewhat related to imagination is humour. We won't say much about humour here – academics writing about humour can be a bit like bishops preaching about sex – but growing up without a sense of humour can be a disadvantage. Of course, some humour can verge on the sarcastic, but the best sort of humour has a number of educationally desirable features: it deflates pomposity, it oils the wheels of social intercourse, it encourages listeners to develop their own wit, and it is enjoyable in its own right.

Equipment for altruism

This third major aim has three elements:

1. moral education in general
2. education for citizenship
3. education for work.

Element 2 is one aspect of element 1, and element 3 is one aspect of element 2.

Moral education

This brings us to another of our major aims: helping children to become morally sensitive people.

It should be clear from the section on links between the aims (see page 8), and from points made elsewhere, that this overlaps with the first general aim, about promoting the student's own well-being. So many personally fulfilling relationships and activities bring with them concern for others' welfare that the two aims are impossible to keep apart.

Moral education is about the nurturing of desirable dispositions, including capacity for moral reasoning and right judgement (Wilson 1990). In this, it follows the same approach as in 'Personal qualities' (see page 23), except that the dispositions it covers are of an altruistic kind. This is not how moral education is always understood. Traditionally, it has often had to do with learning to obey rules about one's moral duties. Parents and teachers have laid it down to children that they must not lie, break promises, or cause harm to others, and that they ought to forgive transgressions against them, to help people in distress, in short, to love their neighbours as themselves (or some other formulation of the Golden Rule). In the religious culture of which we are all still heirs, such injunctions may be thought to emanate from God, in the shape, not least, of God's 'commandments'.

There can be difficulties in this approach. One is that it can leave young people without adequate guidance. Is it all right for them to be moral minimalists, as it were – that is, to hold that they are allowed ruthlessly to pursue their own interests as long as they obey all the rules (refrain from lying, cheating, etc., be generally polite and superficially considerate to others, and lend them a hand if in severe straits)? Or does loving one's neighbour indicate a life altogether more morally strenuous, where one's own interests virtually drop out of the picture?

Basing morality on rules and duties can also be a great generator of guilt. Transgressing a rule is, in its original form, going against the will of God, being left uncertain about what wrath this may incur and how one can atone. Even in the less religious culture that we have inherited, guilt can be a potent emotion in young people, not least over sexual 'transgressions'.

In addition, for those brought up in, or coming to trust in, a more full-bloodedly religious system of moral rules, what happens to their moral outlook if they lose their faith? Have they then no compass left other than self-interest?

A society like our own, in which religious faith in many communities is waning, needs a morality, and a moral education, of a less rule-bound kind, one centred around dispositions.[11] This is not to deny that young children have to know they should not lie, hurt their little sister, or go on yelling when told to stop. But reinforcing these injunctions is, in this alternative view, part of a larger process of building up desirable ways of behaving, feeling, and thinking. Children learn not to hurt their sister partly so as not to incur parental disapproval, partly, and progressively, out of empathy, seeing others as persons who are worthy of respect and with interests comparable to our own. As they learn to do, and to feel, the right things at the right times and in the right circumstances – as with the personal qualities discussed on pages 23–6 – they also gain a fuller understanding of the reasons involved. They see that other people need to be allowed to get on with their own lives; they need respect and recognition, friendliness, politeness, and good humour, as well as sometimes help, sometimes restraint. That is, they come to see others as like themselves. They learn to cooperate with them as equals on a basis of mutual trust. They gain both a clearer picture of what is at issue in conflicts of interest, and also sensitive ways of coping with these. As their little world expands beyond the family, they learn to extend the dispositions they have acquired on a small scale to the larger canvas of neighbourhood, school, the wider society, the world.

Families lay the foundations; schools as well as families build on them. Schools reinforce the dispositions mentioned, helping students, not least, to understand the complexities of the moral world as their horizons enlarge. They complement the work of the family in encouraging children critically to reflect on issues to do with friendships, relations with classmates, school rules, conflicts between authority and autonomy. They celebrate the moral courage to stand up for what one believes is right in the face of counter pressures. They introduce their charges to issues they will confront in the world beyond the school – issues of fairness, protection from harm, and the promotion of people's well-being.

There is much here for the school to do, both in transmitting relevant knowledge and in developing children's ability to discuss these issues in a respectful and increasingly informed way, and coming to see, as they become capable of this, the more general considerations embedded in the particulars. In time, this will involve them in thinking about the bases of morality, its relationship with religion and our social nature, and connections (as well as differences) between the personal and the political. They will also learn to reflect, together and alone, on conflicts and links between their own well-being and other people's, appreciating the many ways in which these overlap (see 'Links between the aims' above).

On pages 17 and 26 we looked at the role of literature in refining children's feelings and deepening their understanding in the area of personal qualities to do with their own flourishing. There is no need to labour the role of stories and dramas, from infancy through to maturity, in also developing *altruistic* sensibilities. The imagination, which can be exercised in all school subjects, not just literature, has a large part to play in moral education, along with the daily routines of school life, knowledge and understanding acquired in various curriculum activities, and, not least, group discussion.

Education for citizenship

This sub-division of the moral aim is that children contribute to civic well-being. This means that they become informed and active citizens of a liberal democratic society (Beck 1998). This in turn requires acquiring certain dispositions on the one hand and certain understandings on the other. As with previous aims, these two aspects are not discrete, in that dispositions are enriched and deepened as understanding grows.

DISPOSITIONS

To begin with dispositions: as just implied, we are dealing with many of the moral virtues discussed above (pages 26–8), appearing now on a civic scale. Fundamental to civic virtues is living together as equal citizens. This has an institutional side in our attachment to the principle of one (adult) person, one vote. But it goes much deeper than electoral arrangements. We express it in our shared concern that everyone be treated as being of equal intrinsic importance. This comes out (or should) in our day-to-day dealings with strangers in the street or on public transport, as much as in the sympathy we feel for those in need in other parts of the community. It matters to us as citizens that every fellow citizen is treated with respect, and is able (or enabled) to lead a flourishing life in his or her own way. This goes with the disposition to stand out against disrespect for this principle of equal consideration – as shown, for instance, in attitudes of social superiority, or actions that make people already badly off even more deprived.

Children can begin to acquire this egalitarian virtue from their earliest years. They learn that they are not the only fish in the pond, that they should not boss their friends, take over their toys, or grab the best food. Once at playgroup or school, if all goes well, they soon accept that they are only one among many. As they grow older, this kind of habituation can be extended to wider spheres, not least via the school as a kind of microcosm of a larger political community.

This discussion of political equality has introduced another political virtue: concern for the well-being of others in the community. Again, this is an everyday moral virtue at work now in a larger sphere. It is shown in our respect for others' freedom to do as they will, as long as they are not harming others – respect for their religious and sexual practices, for instance. It is shown in our willingness to help them to attain the basic requirements of a fulfilling life of their own – in our support for educational, health, and other welfare reforms, for instance. Children's moral education at home will, again, have provided the foundations – and for benevolence not only *within* the national community but also *beyond* it, directed towards the relief of poverty, poor health, and lack of education, and the protection of human rights elsewhere in the world.

Also falling under this heading is concern for the experiences of all sentient beings, such as farm animals and pets, with whom our lives intersect, for the sustainability of the world's resources, for the welfare of human communities facing threats, and for the survival of species as a result of global climate change and the continued growth of the world's human population (Bassey 2011).

To equality, liberty, and benevolence we should add the political virtue of fraternity. This is an underpinning virtue of any community, the social cement that holds it all together. It is not as atomic individuals that citizens fulfil their civic requirements, but as persons bonded together as co-sharers of a political fate. Being born into a family, and before long coming to experience the friendships and cooperative activities of pre-school and school groups, are early steps in acquiring this political virtue.

Central to democracy is a wariness about domination. Given the significance to it of each citizen's personal autonomy, the democrat is on guard against attempts to thwart this – by politicians, for instance, who wish to impose their own ideology on others, or otherwise use state power for their own ends. This manifestation of practical wisdom takes institutional shape in the machinery, for instance, that enables electors periodically to choose and remove governments, but it can be born and can develop in more homely circumstances – in children's reactions to a domineering friend, parent, or teacher, for example. They can and should be brought up in the same wariness towards pressure from the media, advertisers, and other powerful interest groups.

Part of a citizen's repertoire is sensitivity to the complexities of policy-making. Every political decision is many-sided in its likely effects on different people. Budding citizens have to learn to take conflicting considerations into account, to grasp the virtues of compromise, and to avoid the lure of simplistic answers. In this, they extend into the political area what they have learnt about conflict resolution in their own, everyday, personal and moral lives (see page 25 and pages 27–8). In the political sphere, coping with the points to take into account is so much more difficult, partly because of the expertise needed in different areas (economics, law, politics, business, science and technology, etc.). Young people need to come to see this and to realize the dependence of a democratic polity on specialized knowledge. At the same time, they have to learn how to make reasonable judgements about political choices in the absence of possessing such expert understanding themselves. These judgements include ones about how reliable professed experts actually are, and how wary an ordinary citizen needs to be about their pronouncements (Collins and Evans 2007).

To bring home the points in the last paragraph, there should be opportunities for students to participate in the democratic running of the school, in participation in decision-making both within the classroom and in school committees outside it.

A further disposition is attachment to democracy itself. As they grow into its specific values, young people come to see how, despite its imperfections, democracy is worth preserving against the prospect of more oppressive alternatives. This attachment can take different forms. These include:

- endeavouring to keep the democratic ideal vibrant, by welcoming its influence in parts of society not yet under its dominion, not least most workplaces, as well as in certain parts of the world
- active political engagement, for example within a political party, for those so inclined
- willingness to defend their democratic community against attack from within and without.

There is nothing to be said, from a liberal democratic point of view, for inculcating patriotic attitudes, if these are taken as embedding a sense of superiority to other countries; but they are welcome if interpreted as attachment to one's civic community rather than as chauvinism (see Hand 2011). Whether school education for democracy should extend as far as encouraging students to think of themselves as global citizens depends on one's understanding of the term. But there is certainly every reason why, as already suggested, students' political virtues should take them beyond their own national frontiers.

A final word, about discussion, sometimes referred to as 'argumentation'. This is the lifeblood of democratic politics, whether formalized in legislatures or a more ordinary, everyday activity. Our future democratic citizens need to be inducted into its procedures and to gain plenty of experience in it, so that it becomes second nature to them. Most of the topics mentioned in this section, both general and of particular examples, lend themselves to reasoned discussion. This also applies to many of those in the following section. Discussion can, of course, and typically will, take place between individuals in lessons, but schools can facilitate it in other ways. They can set homework so that issues are discussed within families; they can facilitate online debate; they can encourage the development of the capacity for critical reflection, so that students are able, Socratically or otherwise, to debate with each other.

UNDERSTANDING

Acquiring the dispositions just discussed depends on possessing various kinds of understanding, including the notion of democracy itself, and of the values embedded in it. Whereas some older students may attain a reflective, second-order understanding of this territory akin to that found in political philosophy, even very young children can begin to grasp aspects of it in a more tacit and piecemeal way. A typical 5-year-old will know that he or she is not the only person who can have the attention of a teacher, and can grasp the notion of a group's doing what most of its members decide to do.

Understanding democracy also depends on a knowledge of human nature and the constituents of human well-being. This, too, can be expected to deepen as children grow older. They also need, in time, a broad understanding of the institutions of democratic government, including its provision for regular and fair elections, and for law-making, executive, and judicial bodies. In learning to see these institutions as variable embodiments of democratic values, students' attention will constantly be drawn back to the latter and will not dwell only on the mechanisms.

They also need knowledge about the particular geopolitical community in which they live: how large it is, its climate, its main regions and conurbations, its economic life, major areas of public and private provision, significant differences of wealth, religion and community attachments across its area, the role played in its life by mass media and the internet, its relationships with other countries. A grasp of relevant statistics is relevant to these items. To this should be added some understanding of the main currents of global politics, and some historical perspective on how both their own society and the global situation has come to be what it is, as well as on the rise, and sometimes fall, of liberal democratic government over the last three or four centuries. This paragraph overlaps with requirements in the area of education for work (see below).

In the case of the UK, this historical perspective includes some understanding of:

- the change from an agrarian to an industrial society, based first on steam and then on other sources of power
- the rise and fall of the British Empire
- the increase in population and rise of urbanization
- the change from monarchical/aristocratic to democratic government and the rise of liberalism
- changes in the occupational and class structures and their reflection in political changes
- changes in social welfare provision.

Global perspectives include:

- international conflict and moves towards cooperation in Europe and globally
- USA superpower status and the recent rise of newly powerful and rapidly developing economies
- divisions between rich and poor countries
- the spread of democratization and challenges to this
- the depletion of resources and issues of sustainability.

Education for work

INTRODUCTION

This sub-division of the civic aim has largely to do with equipping students to contribute economically to our general well-being. When they enter paid employment, they will also be helping to promote their own well-being, by meeting their basic need for an income. Especially if they are in what are seen as 'better' jobs, they may also be promoting this by using their higher wages to enlarge the range of valuable options that they can afford to engage in, and by enjoying work that is absorbing in itself.

These last two reasons make it a defensible aim of school education to help young people to get the qualifications they need to get a higher-paid and/or intrinsically interesting job. It is a further question what such qualifications might be, and a mistake to assume that the only form they can take is a clutch of good exam results, even less a clutch of good exam results in a canonical list of academic subjects.

One of the distinctive failings of the school examination system in England for many years has been the way in which examinations originally designed for only a small minority of the school population, notably O levels and A levels, have dominated the landscape. Even when some broadening has occurred (notably the introduction of GCSEs and AS levels), a high proportion of successive cohorts are forced through a narrow examination system that suits neither their capabilities nor the needs of employers. The result is an overemphasis on the academic at the expense of the vocational, which ends up disadvantaging those better suited to more vocational subjects and less desk-bound assessment regimes.

At the same time, there are still many jobs that do not need much in the way of school qualifications. The more the school curriculum is orientated towards qualifications, the more questionable is its value to those who do not get them, or who get them but have to make do with a less-skilled job.

WORK-RELATED EDUCATION

Participation in work activities is important in forming positive dispositions that are useful in later life. Since much school learning involves work, this will happen anyway: children learn to plan, organize, and review the work they do; they get used to facing setbacks and overcoming them, and working to deadlines. Cooperative work – on academic, artistic, or other practical projects in democratic participation in class and outside it (see page 29) – is especially important, given that in most jobs people work together. This helps school learners: to distinguish professional relationships with colleagues from more intimate relationships; to enjoy the experience of collaboration; to divide responsibilities; and to fill different roles, for example as leader on some occasions and as the person being led on others. There should also be opportunities for young people to visit workplaces, particularly those to which their families would be unlikely to have access, and take some part in their activities on a 'taster' basis.

As autonomous individuals, most young people will be choosing what work to do in life that is beneficial for all, as well as providing them with an income. Schools should not steer them towards adopting a life-plan, in part because, as we discussed earlier, whether young people live in that way or prefer to take things more as they come should be up to them. As a spur to their autonomy, however, schools should encourage them to discuss and reflect on life-planning as a possible option, as well as the advantages and drawbacks of alternatives.

Also with an eye to students' autonomy, schools will build on what parents do, and on students' everyday experiences, in revealing to them the whole range of occupations open to them, their nature, requirements, chances of securing them, and their likely benefits and disadvantages, both financial and other (Every Child a Chance Trust 2009). As things are, many students, especially those not from families where this kind of information is known and passed on, leave school lacking this overall picture, and hence with limited options.

The school's task is lightened by students' everyday acquaintance with the world of work. They are almost all likely to know something about looking after children, teaching, driving buses, serving in shops, and doing house repairs as well as, or perhaps to a lesser extent, about being a nurse, a professional footballer, or a professional musician. Many will know less about working in the law, finance, the police, the civil service, medical research, journalism, engineering, and construction.

Schools, working with parents, could keep some kind of rough, individualized accounts of what children know and do not know. They would then be in a better position to round out the picture. Schools can also help to challenge children's misapprehensions – beliefs, for instance, that certain kinds of job are not for people of their background, or unrealistic thoughts about their chances of becoming a celebrity. School is also a good place to explore the relationship between work and payment.

Part of learning about the world of work is coming to see how different branches of it relate to people's well-being – their own and others'. Young people should be able to distinguish those kinds of occupation in which one can get wholeheartedly and enjoyably involved from those that are more tedious, so affording fewer opportunities for self-fulfilment (granted that this is a spectrum, and one on which individuals differ). They should also know something about differences of pay and working conditions in different jobs. Young people should know something about the qualifications expected for different kinds of job, as well as the chances of, and strategies for, getting a job they want. This covers information about how much demand there is for recruits, and how much likely competition there is, in this or that field.

Much of this can be learnt from teachers, visiting speakers, textbooks and, not least, projects involving information available electronically and elsewhere. Much, too, can be fed in via the imagination – on the affective as well as on the informational side. We have already seen the importance of the imagination in connection with learning to do with relationships (see page 13), worthwhile activities (pages 14–15), personal qualities (page 26) and morality (page 28). Through listening to or reading fiction and biography, and through watching feature and documentary film material, students can, like the rest of us, pick up a considerable amount about what it is like, and feels like, to work in this field or that.

Class discussion is a good vehicle for sharing perceptions on the attractiveness of different jobs, as well as their downsides, and routes into them. It also helps to open up more general issues about how much income one needs to lead a full life, about fairness, the weight that is put on status, and the conflicts between job demands and time to do other things. At the same time, it is difficult to imagine what doing something day after day is like unless one has tried it for at least one or two days, so imagination and discussion need to be complemented by experience.

Work-related education includes learning about the economy – global as well as national – as a whole, covering such things as:

- the difference between public and private sectors
- global markets
- the role of financial institutions
- competition and monopoly

- advertising
- the allocation of income to wages, investment and dividends
- the role of unions in protecting workers' interests
- political institutions and their part in managing the economy.

Like other aspects of work-related education, this is geared partly to the individual student's own future and partly to his or her moral concern with the well-being of all.

Students need some historical background to make sense of these features of the world of work. This builds on economic aspects of historical work on citizenship (see pages 31–2).

Making sense of the economy depends on seeing its increasing reliance, over time, on applied science and technology, and the mathematics underpinning this. This provides an additional reason for including such subjects in the curriculum. Furthermore, just as we gain skills of utilitarian use for our everyday lives from our study of great literature, notably the ability to read and write, so there are strong extrinsic arguments for students in school to learn a considerable amount of mathematics.

Learners who leave full-time education with limited numeracy skills are severely disadvantaged. They not only end up earning less money on average, but they are less able to make sound judgements about such matters as financial loans (including mortgages), they have difficulties managing household accounts, they have diminished employment opportunities, and they even have poorer health (Every Child a Chance Trust 2009).

However, the evidence that mathematics beyond this level makes a material difference to a person's life circumstances is less convincing. It may be that more advanced study of algebra and geometry is extrinsically valuable, but the jury is still out. This, of course, is not to devalue the worth of studying mathematics for those who wish to (Boaler 2009, Morgan *et al.* 2004). At the same time, there is quite good evidence that there is a shortage in the UK of advanced (A level and above) knowledge and skills in the physical sciences and mathematics, as shown by higher salaries that expertise in these areas brings and by surveys of employers. It has also recently been argued that school IT lessons in the UK generally fail adequately to deal with the subject of computer science (Royal Society 2012).

CONCLUSION

Work-related education is sometimes viewed askance, as of little or no priority in comparison with intellectual and cultural studies pursued for their own sake. There can be an element of self-deception in this, since success in such studies often leads, via higher education, to a 'better' job, and is widely known to do so. The love of academic learning for its intrinsic delights is at the same time instrumentally useful in 'doing well' in the world.

As this section has shown, the truth is that work-related education could well be more prominent in the curriculum than it currently is. It would help to give it more of a practical edge, tied in, as it is, with the other main aims, all of which also have to do with helping the student and others to enjoy a fulfilling life.

Notes

[1] It might be thought that the claim made in the first sentence of this paragraph, that schools have no hand in providing income, needs to be qualified in light of their obvious role, as things are now, in helping students to get the qualifications they need for further and higher education and the better-paid jobs to which these often lead. We say more about this below, since it is more relevant to work-related aims than to basic needs aims. In the present section, the claim is simply that the learning promoted by the school does not *in itself* provide students with the basic income they will need.

[2] On the relationship between personal flourishing and work, see White (2011a), 68–76.

[3] The three decades from the 1960s saw many rival ventures of this sort.

[4] We ignore sudoko and other number puzzles, since, although these require an acquaintance with numbers up to nine, they make few demands on the world of mathematics beyond this.

[5] Not that more popular literature has *no* place in education, or even in compulsory classes. It may be there, for instance, for motivational reasons.

[6] Literature, not English (or other mother tongue) literature only. Chekhov in translation is as fit for the purposes discussed in the text as Austen or Steinbeck. Nor do we confine our point to reading; most people gain more from watching and listening to plays than from reading them.

[7] Two of the welcome features of the 2011 report from the Expert Panel for the National Curriculum review, published by the Department for Education, London (https://www.education.gov.uk/publications/eOrderingDownload/NCR-Expert%20Panel%20Report.pdf (accessed 15 January 2012)), are that it distinguishes between what a national curriculum should specify and what a school should provide and that it attempts to provide reasons as to which subjects should be compulsory to age 16 and which not.

[8] It would be good if students did not have to take up these options at one specified time only, but could sign up for them at any of various points in their school career.

[9] Watching drama should be included along with reading literature.

[10] Including geography which, of course, also encompasses other modes of study. See Lambert, D. and Morgan, J. (2010) *Teaching Geography 11–18: A conceptual approach* (Maidenhead: Open University Press).

[11] This is not to imply that all religious moral education is rules-focused rather than disposition-focused.

Part 2

Aims into practice

Michael Reiss and John White

Introduction

Part 1 has described how an aims-based curriculum functions and what makes it different from a subject-based one. It has shown how important it is to work out the most general aims carefully and at some length. This is the most difficult part of the project, on which all else depends. Once it is in place, the next step – deriving aims of increasing specificity – is, as we have seen, more straightforward.

There can be aims-based curricula of many sorts, but an appropriate one for a country like England and similar places is one tailored to the values of a liberal democracy. This is the kind we have developed here. We put it forward as a more acceptable way of framing a national curriculum than the subject-based one we have at present.[1]

This book is not a piece of political policy-making. It does not aim at producing a detailed scheme that can replace the National Curriculum programmes we use now in England and Wales. We acknowledge that politics has to be realistic. It cannot take a blueprint from the shelf and immediately set about applying it. Policy-makers have to work from where things are now and make all kinds of compromises on the way to getting closer to an ideal.

Yet unless they have some sort of picture of an alternative to the status quo, they cannot sensibly change it. That is why we have seen it as our primary task in this book to paint in the main features of this picture – and as starkly as its unavoidable complexities allow. This primary task is now complete.

We now turn to related matters. In 'Generating more specific aims' below, we give some indication of how the aims-based process, moving from general to more specific aims, can continue further. It would not be appropriate in a short book to do this in all the aims-areas that we have opened up so far. We are not writing a complete taxonomy of aims, but delineating an as yet unfamiliar concept – that of an aims-based curriculum – in the broadest of strokes. We want, nevertheless, to show, with one or two examples, how things can go further.

Showing this is important if an aims-based approach is to replace a subject-based construction of a national curriculum – in England or anywhere else. It underlines that aims need not remain at a very general level, but can become as specific as any curriculum-making – at national, local, or school level – would require.

The brief 'Overlapping aims' section also has practical purposes in mind. It is about overlaps and how to deal with them. An aims-based approach – ours is an example – is likely to lead to similar aims occurring in different parts of the structure. In our scheme, there is an overlap, for instance, between the large-scale historical understanding of humanity nurtured in background studies and the history of one's own community required by civic aims. How best to cope with this in students' learning?

The section 'Implementing a fully aims-based approach' is much longer, and has several sub-divisions. It seeks to answer the sceptical question: 'An aims-based approach may be fine in theory, but however could it be implemented?' This can be taken in more than one way. In this section we outline an administrative structure within which a *fully* aims-based curriculum could operate. We look at the division of responsibility between the political and professional spheres, give a thumbnail sketch of how schools might operate an aims-based curriculum, and look at implications for assessment, inspection, and teacher supply.

This may still not be enough for the hard-nosed national policy-maker who has, as we said above, to begin with where we are now and take practical steps to turn this status quo into something more defensible. In 'Facing political realities', drawing on previous attempts to move policy in an aims-based direction, we offer a number of specific suggestions to take things further.

This is followed by concluding remarks about the enterprise as a whole.

Generating more specific aims

The aims discussed so far cover the dispositions and kinds of understanding that, we argue, it would be good for every learner to possess in an enduring way. The dispositions are habits of behaviour and feeling that draw on personal and moral qualities, as well as capabilities for aesthetic response, and basic skills of literacy and numeracy. These dispositions bring with them, as we have seen, all kinds of demands on understanding.

We have also discussed other capabilities, not so tied, at least for every learner, to enduring dispositions. Take modern foreign language learning. As things are now, many school students learn to speak and write some French, Spanish, Mandarin, etc. But only some of them – those living for long periods abroad, for instance, or employed as translators – will use those skills on a habitual basis in later life. In our own scheme (page 19), we have suggested that students be given a taster course in one or more foreign languages, to see if they wish to pursue such study as an optional activity over a longer period, perhaps for some years. As we also saw in that section, there are many other skills of this sort that only some learners will use in later life, but which all should have some opportunity to acquire on a taster/option basis: such things as higher mathematical procedures, the skills of specialized sports, artistic skills in performance or creation, and other practical skills in areas like gardening, care of animals, design, and construction.

We are, of course, aware that any attempt to make optional a subject that has previously been mandatory in a curriculum leads immediately to a passionate defence of what it is that is about to be 'lost'. Members of Parliament and the general public are regaled with dire predictions of what will come to pass nationally, once such and such a subject is 'dropped'. The result is a curriculum that becomes increasingly full, during the years of compulsory education, with yet more subjects. As new subjects (e.g. ICT, citizenship, earth sciences) are added, the curriculum either becomes overloaded or some existing subjects slowly and painfully die in terms of curriculum time through successive 'salami slicing'.

There are several problems with such an approach. For one thing, it is excessively conservative. We end up with a curriculum still shaped by arguments of a century or more ago. For another, it underestimates learners. It is no longer the case, if it ever was, that one's only chance of learning (or learning about) German, matrices, ballet, or how to service a car is in a school lesson. There are no critical periods for such matters – one really can pick them up later in life, as and when needed or desired.

We will be saying more below (on page 53) about the place of optional activities in school. For the moment, however, we focus on the dispositions and understanding that every young person will need for a life of personal and civic well-being, and that schools can help them to acquire.

In the sphere of knowledge and understanding, it is easier than with dispositions to locate more determinate aims than those we have already outlined. It is hard to see what might be a sub-aim of cooperativeness, say, or perseverance. This is not to say that nothing further can be said about them in guidance to teachers; only that, given such a gloss, it is reasonably straightforward for teachers to know how to go about encouraging them.

It would be impossible for us to specify in more detail every kind of knowledge-aim. This book is not a National Curriculum handbook for teachers. It cannot hope to spell out all the knowledge-aims required across the board in non-optional school education. It will have achieved its own aim if it has shown, in broader outline than this, how an aims-based curriculum is to be constructed, beginning from very general objectives and moving towards the specific aims recommended at national level for all students.

At the same time, our book will not fully achieve its own aim without some *indication*, albeit not a comprehensive survey, of aims at this more determinate level. It may be helpful, therefore, if we give a few examples. We revisit three of the aims from Part 1, one in the area of history and the other two in the fields of science, mathematics, and technology.

Background aims: historical understanding

As part of their background understanding of the human world, we suggested (page 11) that learners need to know something about:

> the main features of human prehistory and history, from earliest human
> life through the coming of agriculture and city life to the invention of
> printing, the rise of global trade, the arrival of industrialization and
> mechanization, and our own increasingly knowledge-based age.

The background aims, of which these form a part, look at human life and the world in which it takes place in their broadest contours. This suggests that we see both early and later human development against the backdrop of our animal nature and evolution from other species. It draws attention to such things as our perennial struggles to possess food, shelter and other basic necessities of survival and reproduction, aspects of our social nature that lead us to work together in providing them, as well as more competitive aspects of our make-up connected with domination and submission. Within such a framework, students need a broad-brush picture of what is known about human prehistory, especially about timescales; changes from a hunter-gatherer economy to one based on agriculture; the movement and distribution of human communities across the globe and their adaptation to different climatic conditions and natural resources; and the significance of language in human life and the formation of the major language groups.

The timeline is continued into the last few thousand years covered by historical records. Stages along it include:

- the rise of early civilizations in China, India, the Middle East, Greece, Rome, Africa, the Americas, and elsewhere
- the growth of major world religions, including Judaism, Christianity, Islam, Buddhism, and Hinduism
- the use of money in the rise of commerce
- the Renaissance and the Reformation
- the increasing importance of printing
- advances in navigation, global trade, and the formation of national states and empires in Europe in the sixteenth and seventeenth centuries
- the coming of industrialization, its changing dependence on different sources of power and different technologies, from the age of steam to the age of electronics
- increasing urbanization and changes in living conditions, including food, shelter, transport, education, working conditions
- rises in population and pressure on global resources
- international economic links and competition
- the rise and fall of empires from those of Britain, France, and Spain to the USA and the BRIC economies (Brazil, Russia, India, and China)
- the challenge to authoritarian forms of governance from liberal and democratic ideas and movements.

This list is no doubt incomplete, but it gives some idea of what an educated person should ideally be expected to know something about, at least in broad outline. Of course, there will be some differences from one country to another, precisely because our argument here is about the fulfilment of the background aims; each person's background, even in an increasingly global world, depends on where they live.

Michael Reiss and John White

This is not to say that there should be a comprehensive coverage of all these topics while one is still at school. In some cases, signposts will do: if a central school aim is to make students enthusiastic about learning and eager to continue their explorations once school is behind them, they will be able to get a long way on their own, given that their teachers have pointed the way. This is especially true in the age of the internet, provided that learners are equipped to navigate it for this purpose.

This point can be generalized from prehistorical and historical studies to many other aims on our list. It brings us back to the dangers, mentioned earlier (pages 39–40), of thinking of the curriculum in terms of a comprehensive list of items, all of which have to be covered. Gaps in knowledge are not so important, as long as school leavers have some idea of what these gaps are and how they could fill them later. In any case, the topics or items on a curriculum are not important in themselves. This is to place too much emphasis on their discreteness, and risks losing from sight what is surely more valuable: the bearing of a topic on the wider whole of which it forms a part. What is central in these 'timeline' studies is that the student understands something of the great sweep of human development, its deviations from – as well as progress towards – a fulfilling life for all. The story of the early irrigation of the Nile area, or of Magellan's circumnavigation of the world, may or may not come within a particular learner's experience. What is more important is that schools encourage students to connect knowledge, to see parts in relation to wholes.

In the case of prehistory and history, these connections also extend to other aims in our overall aims framework – to understanding the world of nature (via the link with the evolution of life forms); basic human needs and their bearing on flourishing; human nature as represented in literature; cooperativeness and other moral values; citizenship aims to do with liberal democratic values and global interconnectedness; economic understanding.

Background aims: scientific, mathematical, and technological understanding

The second example is also about background aims – in this case, about the more specific understanding of science, mathematics, and technology that these require.

As far as the sciences go, perhaps above all they help us to situate ourselves both temporally and spatially in the world in which we live. It is clear that the universe is almost unimaginably old – some 13.6 billion years is the current consensus – and that there are literally many billions of stars, a high proportion of them with planets of their own. In one sense, then, science tells us that our own world is not that special. And yet we still do not know whether our planet alone is home to life.

Science proceeds through the objective testing of hypotheses about our material world. The growth in scientific knowledge gives us greater understanding of that world. Thanks to science, there is, for instance, no need for people to be superstitious or to fear witchcraft. Tsunamis and infectious diseases – still, sadly, all too often with attendant human misery and loss of life – are not the result of individual wickedness. We can better direct our guilt and shame towards those undesirable features of the world for which we do have moral responsibility.

School coverage of the sciences should therefore include something about what is generally referred to as 'the nature of science', i.e. how scientific knowledge is arrived at and its limits. For example, science tells us much about why the world is as it is, not what we should do in it. In addition, certain core scientific material should be included:

- the particulate theory of matter
- the difference between elements, atoms, and molecules
- the germ origins of much disease
- the evidence for evolution
- the importance of natural selection
- the way in which the structures of organisms are related to how they function
- the interrelationships between organisms and their environments
- the relationship between electricity and magnetism
- certain basic laws of physics, such as the conservation of mass, the conservation of energy, and the second law of thermodynamics
- the importance of gravitational and other forces
- the role of plate tectonics.

As we have already argued (on pages 17–18), mathematics has but a modest claim for inclusion in the mandatory curriculum on the grounds of its contribution to meeting the background aims (see Hacker 2012). Nevertheless, a certain understanding of mathematics helps in this regard. We are not thinking only of the fact that such everyday activities as shopping (basic addition, subtraction, multiplication, and division; percentages; ratios; approximation) and using a map (scales, directions) require a certain amount of mathematics. Perhaps less obviously, to be able to think mathematically, especially when combined with knowledge from other subjects, is to be able to engage more richly in much 'what if?' thought, with the potential to benefit both ourselves and others. How important for my health is it for me not to be 10 per cent underweight or overweight? How much greener is it for me to take the train from London to Edinburgh rather than to fly? Is it worth taking advantage of yet another introductory offer from a mobile phone operator? Should we vaccinate our children using the MMR vaccine?

It is particularly difficult to make generalizations about those aspects of technology that should be included, as this is strongly context-specific. For example, we might want students to know something of how food is produced, but whether they should know about arable crops, farm animals, or horticulture depends on time or place.

More generally, though, technology differs in two important regards from both science and mathematics: it is intimately concerned with both aesthetics and morality. To decide, for example, what a good home, transport system, source of energy, or computer is, requires far more interdisciplinary thinking than is required by science or mathematics.

Work-related aims: scientific, mathematical, and technological understanding

Our third example is also about these three areas – science, mathematics, and technology – but now we look at these in relation to the world of work.

We stated earlier (on page 35) that in order to make sense of national and global economies, students have to grasp the increasing reliance of these economies, over time, on 'applied science and technology, and the mathematics underpinning this'. This is important to them both as citizens and, more personally, in gaining a better understanding of the range of jobs from which they can choose. While mathematics and technology have been around for millennia and 'modern' science for at least several hundred years, it is clear that the proportion of jobs that rely on these subjects has increased in recent decades. Indeed, it seems to be the endless lament of Western governments that we aren't producing enough university science, technology, engineering, and mathematics (STEM) graduates (European Commission 2004, National Academy of Sciences Committee on Science Engineering and Public Policy 2007).

Of course, it is difficult to predict whether such shortages of STEM graduates (and others who work in STEM fields, e.g. as technicians) will continue. Perhaps increasing developments in automation will mean that many STEM jobs will no longer exist just as, in past times, first agricultural and then industrial employment rose and fell. Nevertheless, STEM graduates are presently in short supply in many countries (as evidenced by the higher earnings they typically obtain once in post).

How, though, should one decide, for such possible employment purposes, how much and what sort of science, technology, engineering, and mathematics students should experience when at school? The first principle, surely, should be to provide sufficient material for students to be reasonably well informed when deciding whether or not to continue with the subject for career reasons, once it becomes optional. This argues against the need for comprehensive coverage; what is needed, rather, is what we have previously referred to as 'tasters' (page 18). Furthermore, a significant proportion of this material should be 'applied', so as to indicate the uses to which such knowledge is put. Indeed, not only should it be applied, but courses should also indicate how people make use of it in employment.

To give just one example, when teaching the topic of digestion, say to 13-year-olds, one might include material on how such knowledge is used by dieticians and others working with people who have cystic fibrosis (a condition associated, among other symptoms, with poor absorption of nutrients from the gut), with elite cyclists (who typically consume about 6,000 calories a day during events such as the Tour de

France), and with pregnant women (where eating for two does not mean eating twice as much and where morning sickness can complicate matters).

However, despite attempts to introduce more applied material into a number of science and mathematics courses, such material is often considered of lower intellectual worth than 'pure' science and mathematics. Such an attitude, aside from being narrow-minded, is probably counterproductive; some students are attracted by learning material that they can see might lead to satisfying employment. In any event, the relationship between pure and applied science is not simply a one-way relationship, in which pure knowledge leads to applied knowledge. As historians and sociologists of science now accept, the relationship is more complicated than that. In some cases, advances in the applied sciences lead to advances in pure sciences.[2]

Conclusion

These are three examples of how an aims-based curriculum can lead into specifics. We have not gone so far as to prescribe in detail what national expectations should be in these areas. This turns partly on deciding what should be laid down nationally and what should be left to schools. We come back to this in 'Division of responsibility: state and school' below. But our sights go beyond school learning. They extend to what an educated person can be reasonably expected to be like – to the dispositions he or she should possess, and the understandings that these bring in their train. For none of us is this formation complete when we finish school. A new national curriculum should begin with this wide-angled picture and not expect schools to complete it. Central to schools' task is that their leavers should have the desire to learn more. For them, this is an attainment target incalculably more important than knowing about the Crimean War or tangents and cosines.

This brings us back to the primacy of dispositions. To follow up a remark we made above, it is easier to go into specifics about knowledge-aims than about personal qualities. The paragraphs above about background aims in history (see page 40) could easily be expanded three- or fourfold so as to include finer-grained objectives; but what sub-divisions might we make in dispositions like friendliness or wholeheartedness of involvement?

This easier divisibility of knowledge-aims makes them an ideal focus for a certain brand of curriculum-making. If you are looking for programmes that are well stocked with items that a teacher can tick off and that are easily assessible, here is an obvious source. This may be one factor in the success of the largely knowledge-based traditional curriculum, of which the English National Curriculum is one example among hundreds around the world. Certainly, if we study the historical origins of this kind of curriculum, we find an interest in the logical subdivision of knowledge part of this story from the mid-sixteenth century onwards (White 2011b: chs 2, 3).

Knowledge is central to any decent education, as we hope our own aims-based scheme has abundantly illustrated. But it has to know its place. As we have by now no need to labour, it should be subordinate to the personal qualities that we want students to possess. 'Content' is not the heartland of the curriculum. The centre to which everything in it must always be returning is the sort of people we want our students to become.

Overlapping aims

This same message should be borne in mind as we turn to overlaps between aims found in different parts of the overall structure. Here are some examples.

As we saw in the previous section, there is a scientific component both to background aims (to do with understanding the kinds of creature that human beings are, and the main features of the biological and physical worlds we live in), and also to the understanding of the economic basis of our society included under civic and work aims. Science also appears under personal aims to do with intrinsically worthwhile activities, to be studied for its own sake, partly on an optional basis. It also weaves in and out of other aims, including personal ones to do with health-related dispositions and with sex and relationships education. Social science aims that are to do with diversity and other features of our national community also appear among civic aims.

There is a historical dimension to background aims, as elaborated in 'Generating more specific aims' above. This deals with broad perspectives on the history of human beings. Civic aims include a more localized concern with the history of one's national community and with a historical background to global politics. As with the sciences, history can be a personally worthwhile activity pursued out of intrinsic interest, especially for students wishing to take it further as an option. As with the sciences, too, historical perspectives can illuminate a range of other aims – from changes in working conditions to changes in eating patterns, how we see morality, attitudes towards sex.

Similar points can be made about mathematics. Basic arithmetic is a prerequisite in innumerable aims across the whole range. Statistics comes into civic aims. Much school science requires a certain level of mathematical capability. Indeed, there is a growing consensus that England allows too many students to drop mathematics at age 16 and that for a wide range of subjects, not just the sciences, continued study of mathematics is beneficial (Hodgen and Pepper 2010). We have also suggested that mathematics as something to be pursued for its own sake can be studied on a taster/option model.

Literature and other arts are prominent among the intrinsically worthwhile aims of a personal sort. The prominence of creative industries in national life and more extensively brings arts-related aims into civic education and education for work. At innumerable points, moral aims and background reflection on humanity and its relation to the universe deal with perennial preoccupations of literature and other arts, particularly the visual arts.

Personal aims also find echoes elsewhere. We have already drawn attention to the inseparability of personal well-being and altruism (page 8). Autonomy is prominent in related forms: making informed choices among worthwhile activities, relying on one's own judgement in moral matters, being critically aware on the intellectual front. Basic needs feature both as an element in personal well-being and as a focal point of civic and economic life.[3] Myths about human nature on the personal front, in relationships between the sexes, for instance, or to do with perceived differences in ability, connect with political and social mythologies about differences between nationalities and ethnic groups.

These examples are not exhaustive. The presence of overlaps prompts questions about how the aims are best pursued in school programmes. Take, for instance, the overlapping historical aims. Are these best promoted together in discrete history lessons, or separately – in ways more directly connected to the wider aims under which they fall?

We doubt whether there is any one best way of proceeding – and would prefer to leave it to schools to decide, here and more generally, what kind of curriculum organization suits them best according to circumstances. Whichever route is followed, however, it must remain in close contact with the relevant wider aims and with the basic values of the whole aims-structure. It may sometimes be easier to do this via interdisciplinary projects and themes that centre around these wider aims than by discrete teaching within a standard subject (see below, page 54). Work to do with the history of humanity may, for instance, be included in a series of projects on human nature, approaching this from biological, religious, and other perspectives as well as historical ones. This would not rule out making connections with more particular, for example national, histories. On the contrary, these should be welcomed. We can imagine, for instance, industrialization as a salient feature in the story of human beings as a whole being linked with the Industrial Revolution in Britain. As with Danny Boyle's remarkable portrayal in the 2012 Olympics opening ceremony of the replacement of rural Britain by a land of furnaces and chimneys, this would help students to see domestic events not as discretely British, but as instances of something of more general human significance.

If, as we hope, our present subject-based curriculum morphs into an aims-based one, the existence of such overlaps may be helpful in moving things on. Religious education, for instance, is a protected subject at the moment. Its non-statutory national framework, intended for the 500 or so periods of RE normally occurring in a student's school life, is problematic in many ways: it too often fills much of this time with excessive details of practices and beliefs within the major faiths; makes insufficient room for critical discussion of central religious claims, like the claim that God exists; leaves non-religious perspectives non-mandatory; and may embody an unconscious bias towards a religious point of view in the very weight of its preoccupation with intra-faith details and its too frequent association of moral issues with religion.

From an aims-based viewpoint, there are at least two obvious places where religion comes into the picture: in background discussion of ultimate questions (see pages 9 and 12), and in the understanding of social diversity, including religious diversity, that falls under citizenship aims. To these may be added some understanding of the religious framework necessary for a full appreciation of literature, history, the visual arts, and music.

In this way, adopting an aims-based standpoint may be of service to curriculum reformers within RE who, while still keeping religious education as part of the school's offering, are keen to refashion the status quo into something more rationally defensible. We see such a development as a possible stepping stone to a more fully aims-based curriculum. Similar points can be made about transitions in other current subject areas.

Implementing a fully aims-based approach

The case for, and limits of, state control

What education should be for is essentially a political issue, since it is intimately connected with the kind of society we wish to bring about or maintain. In a liberal democracy of equal citizens, teachers and other educators have no special, privileged voice on this. Those who deliver our post, those who spend their time bringing up young children, shopkeepers, and pensioners have the same stake as any educator.

The proper role of the state is to determine what the aims of schools should be, from the most general ones down to where schools are left to decide on more specific ones (see 'Division of responsibility: state and school' below). It should not be up to a government temporarily in power to impose its own idiosyncratic views about what these aims should be, still less its prejudices about how these should be taught. A liberal democratic society, in which every citizen is treated as of equal worth, should have a mechanism in place to ensure that aims are in line with and promote such a society.

This speaks in favour of establishing some kind of commission, protected from political meddling, to act as trustee for a defensible national curriculum. Its task should be to work out a unified set of aims befitting our liberal democracy, stretching from general to specific (New Visions for Education Group 2010).

Following extensive public consultation, within and without the teaching profession, such a commission would painstakingly consider what the aims should be and set out a rational defence of the ones it selects and their interconnections. After further thorough public discussion of these, the commission should make recommendations to the secretary of state on a final version that would provide national guidelines for all schools, including private schools, academies, and free schools. This should be accompanied by a full rationale. For schools and teachers, this would be better than a mere list of aims, such as we have now. It would help them to understand how the aims are to be taken, how they interrelate.

There is a case for removing the statutory status of the National Curriculum so that it became, as in Scotland, a non-mandatory guide to what the nation expects of all its schools. This would be less costly and less time-consuming, as well as helping to wean teachers off habits of uncritical compliance and to become more imaginative in responding to the needs of their students.

Non-statutory guidance would not be a return to the pre-1988 system of professional control, with the excessive school autonomy that sometimes went with this. Schools could not simply ignore it. The aims of the school curriculum, but not their implementation, would be determined at the political level, and schools would be required to have regard to them. If they departed from them, they would have to be able – and this is the key point – to justify such departure. Non-statutory guidance allied to an inspection system has much of the force of a statutory curriculum, but if setting it aside leads to good performance, the decision to do something different becomes beyond criticism – so there is genuine freedom to experiment for schools that are performing well.

Finally, the commission would not be a quango continuously in session; that would be both costly and unnecessary. It would be expected to review the national aims perhaps every five years; and there would be no changes to them between reviews. It should see the aims, deriving as they do from the principles by which we live as a democratic people, as something like part of our (unwritten) constitution. Like other parts of this, an independent judiciary for instance, our national aims need protection from arbitrary executive power. That is not to say that they cannot be changed from time to time, but these changes should no longer be at the whim of politicians.

Division of responsibility: state and school

The state should decide the most general aims and the more general sub-aims that fall under them. At some point in this process of increasing specification it has to hand over responsibility to the school. Are there any general considerations that help us to see where this point should be?

In 'Generating more specific aims' above, we mentioned the familiar truth that a person's education is not complete when he or she leaves school. The more detailed the specification of aims becomes, the more likely it is that many of them will not be attained, or only imperfectly attained, by school-leaving age. This is especially true of aims concerning breadth of understanding. There will also be wide variations, of course, among individuals.

Given this, one way forward would be for the state to lay down a list of aims and sub-aims in each area in a few paragraphs of detail. These would be ideal attainments for every citizen. Especially because covering the ground is not the paramount consideration (see pages 39–40 above), schools would not be expected to achieve all these aims in depth for all their students, but *would* be expected to have introduced students to them, so that they can see their place in the larger picture. Schools would also be tasked with putting school leavers on appropriate paths to take things further. It would be one responsibility of the commission mentioned above (in 'The case for, and limits of, state control') to reach agreement on where the state–school boundary should be set in each aims-area, and to adjust this boundary from time to time.

In a system like England's, where pupils usually change schools about halfway through their school career, it would make sense for the state, again in the form of the commission, roughly to indicate national expectations by the age of 11. Some of the items in the aims-structure we outlined earlier have a natural place in primary schooling – basic literacy, for instance, and arithmetic. Others – assessing arguments for and against the existence of God, for instance, or reflection on the basic values of liberal democracy – will be explored in depth only at secondary level.

If we stay with this last example, it reminds us that we do not typically learn things completely item by item, but deepen our experience or understanding over time. Children in the first years of primary school may indeed not be able to talk abstractly about the civic values of tolerance, cooperativeness, and equality; but they can be, and in good primary schools are (Swann *et al.* 2012), engaged in cooperative projects in which they are encouraged to treat everyone else with decency and respect. In this way they learn what liberal democratic virtues are in practice, gradually gaining more ability to articulate them as their conceptual grasp grows.

This gradual deepening of understanding is a feature of all fields of worthwhile learning – of appreciation of art or a grasp of mathematics as well as of assimilating personal and moral virtues. It is the conceptual truth underlying Jerome Bruner's well-known advocacy of 'the spiral curriculum' (Bruner 1960: 52). It also urges us – and any commission setting national expectations for what primary schooling can achieve – to put considerable store by how deeply children have entered into this aims-area or that, and not to put undue weight on mere breadth of coverage.

It would also be helpful to extend the present practice in England of curricular collaboration between the primary schools in a town or other such area and the smaller number of local secondary schools. In this way the secondary schools that are taking over the baton will have a much more fine-tuned awareness than any national guidelines can give them of where their new intakes from the primary schools are in their learning.

Countries with all-through schools, that is, without this division between primary and secondary stages, do not face this issue.

The scope of national aims

The liberal democratic aims of this aims-based curriculum are intended for every young citizen of a liberal democracy. They are, therefore, meant to apply to all its schools. This seems an unexceptionable claim, and so it should be. In England, however, it presents a stiff challenge to the status quo.

When introduced in 1988, the National Curriculum, which our aims-based scheme has been designed to replace, covered all state-maintained schools, but private schools were exempt. After 2000, the secondary 'academies' created by the Labour Government especially in more deprived areas were not subject to the National Curriculum apart from the three core subjects of English, mathematics, and science. In 2010, the Coalition Government began greatly to expand the academy programme and 45 per cent of secondary schools have already joined it (by August 2012), as well as a number of primaries. 'Free schools', also introduced by the Coalition, are also able to have their own curriculum.

Current policies are chipping away at, not to say undermining, the idea of nationwide curriculum expectations. Higher status and privilege in the school world are increasingly associated with freedom from such constraints.

Freedom for what? For those who control the curriculum of private schools, free schools, and academies to impose their own preferences in lieu of democratically decided ones. These controllers include: the leaders of private schools, influenced by the parents who are their clients; creators of free schools; and sponsors of academies.

In 'The case for, and limits of, state control' above, we argued that in a liberal democracy of equal citizens, teachers have no special, privileged voice on the basic aims of school curricula. Because what schools do affects the kind of society we are co-creating, we are all entitled to a say in what they should be working towards. In a representative democracy, this points to some kind of political control; we have already stated the case for this being at one remove from ministerial rule, for example in the shape of a national commission.

Teachers have a strong case for determining how their school's aims should be implemented. They, not government ministers or anyone else (though governors should play their part), know best the circumstances within which they work, including the kind of students they teach and the local communities from which these come. But teachers, as a section of the total citizenry, have no privileged voice on what schools should be for.

Heads of private schools, the parents behind them, and academy sponsors are equally only sectional voices. Parents may seem to be on stronger ground. Is it not one's right, as a parent, to influence how one's child is to grow up? And does this not cover being able to choose a school with goals and an ethos fitting one's own values and beliefs?

We commonly take parents' rights – their moral rights, not their rights in law – as read. But what is the rational basis for them? If parents owned their children, they would perhaps be on strong ground in deciding what should become of them. But the parent–child relationship is not one of ownership. Do parents have the right to bring children up in the mores and beliefs of their community, based on their (the parents') duty to the community to do so? Does the implied or explicit promise to bring up their children as good Catholics or Muslims trump the principle that the children should in time make up their own minds as to how they will lead their lives? If, as in this book, we are working within the framework of a liberal democratic society, this entails treating the personal autonomy of the citizen as a core value. There is no good reason why some other person – a parent, a priest, a charismatic leader, or anyone else – should direct one's life.

Parents do not have the right, just because they are parents, to determine how their child is to be educated. The child, on the other hand, *does* grow into the right to determine the shape of his or her own life. This does not mean that parents have *no* rights in the area of children's education, but what rights they have are not self-justifying, but based on their *responsibilities* as parents (White 1994). If, for instance, some officious neighbour tried, unbidden, to have a hand in the upbringing of their toddler, the parent would have the moral right to stop them. This is at least in part because one of the responsibilities of a parent is to see that a young child is brought up within a consistent pattern of expectations, and the busybody's interference is a threat to this.

In a liberal democracy, another of the responsibilities of the parent is to see that their child is brought up within its core values, of personal autonomy, equality of respect, and cooperation in the common interest. These are central values in the aims-based curriculum that we have outlined. If parents are to have the right to send their children to private schools,[4] these can only be schools whose educational programme has not been fashioned in line with the preferences of this or that individual or group, but which is built around aims democratically determined. This does not imply that there can be *no* community-based input into the curriculum. On the contrary, if being brought up partly within, say, a Jewish or Muslim community is likely to contribute to a child's flourishing, this provides a good liberal democratic reason to take this into consideration in schooling arrangements, as long as this is within the framework of preparation for autonomous living in a wider society (Raz 1994: 155–76). If schools have a community orientation of this sort, they cannot be exempt from having to follow the nationally laid-down aims to which other schools have to abide.

Aims-based planning within the school

Teachers, as we said above, are best placed to implement a national aims-based scheme according to local circumstances to do with their students, the school's resources, the surrounding community, etc. For all these teachers, the more general aims and sub-aims are the first object of their attention. These aims are what bind together all teachers in a school, whatever their own special interests. The more room there is for collective thinking across the school staff about how to embed these aims in the school's daily practices, the more able the school is to keep to its core purposes.

Take as an example one of the background aims that we discussed under 'Making the aims more determinate' on page 11:

> Part of this self- and other-understanding is about not being imprisoned within contested beliefs about human beings that may hinder one's own and others' flourishing. These may include the belief that we all have individually differing limits of intellectual ability, as well as myths – often related to this – about class-based, religious, gender-related, national or ethnic superiority and inferiority.

A school that is sceptical about the idea of such limits to intellectual ability (except in the case, for instance, of some students with a brain injury) will build in practices that reflect this. It will look askance at setting and streaming arrangements that reinforce in some students the notion that they are not very bright and cause others to preen themselves on their superior intelligence. It will set its face against simplistic 'gifted and talented' programmes. It will even be wary of using the language of 'mixed ability' classes, where, again, this term may suggest individual limits of innate intelligence.

Positively, a school committed to 'learning without limits', like Wroxham primary school in Potters Bar, Hertfordshire, will be constantly reinforcing this principle across everything it does. It is likely to favour a large measure of collective as well as individual learning, building 'a learning community', and 'encouraging children to support and help one another'.[5]

Making curriculum activities relevant, meaningful, and enjoyable will encourage learners to get caught up in what they are doing and strengthen their belief, bolstered by the school's leitmotif, that they can learn whatever they want to. This will also promote another of the aims in the scheme we have proposed (see page 15):

> ... if part of what schools should be preparing students for is lives of enthusiastic engagement in valuable activities, what better way of doing this than by filling their school day, as far as realistically possible, with activities that they find enjoyable and wholly absorbing, and in which they can find success?

Many of these activities are likely to be collaborative, as we have suggested. Where they are not only collaborative but also unconcerned about remaining strictly within traditional subject boundaries, they can be useful vehicles for attending to a number of the more specific, as well as more general, aims in an aims-based scheme at the same time.

An example from St John's Community School in Marlborough makes the point. As part of RSA's Opening Minds project, the school recently devoted part of its Year 7 timetable to a lengthy project called 'Going Places'. Here:

> … the story starts with an introduction into travel and why people move from place to place both historically and today. Stereotyping, customs and styles of world music become enmeshed in journeys through time, the crusades, basic navigation, finding the way using co-ordinates, folk tales, castles and medieval invasions, ballads, and pilgrimages. The journey visits China, India and Italy and ends at the outer limits with a vision of the universe of Stephen Hawking. En-route the students will have built siege engines, used algebra, investigated forces, movement and power; they will have met Leonardo da Vinci and discussed his scientific inventions.
>
> (St John's Marlborough n.d.)

Collaborative learning not only has the potential to make learning more enjoyable: it can also mirror in microcosm the virtues of living together in a liberal democratic community. At Wroxham School, the collaboration extends over age, with older children often involved in activities with younger ones. These include weekly, mixed-age, circle meetings that give every child a voice to express their ideas and participate in decisions to improve their lives in the school. Everybody is included in the circle, not only the children, but also all the adults working in the school, including teaching assistants and volunteers (Swann *et al.* 2012: 16). One idea that children brought up in this way at Wroxham had was to alleviate the school's shortage of library space by buying an old double-decker bus and converting it for this purpose. It now stands in the school grounds, gaily painted in a design produced by the children, and with plenty of comfortable spaces for learners to browse and read.

If students are to be brought up as participating members of a democracy, of a society in which everyone treats others as equals, it is important to break down the many barriers to this, especially in a status-ridden country like England. While keeping their directive role in close collaboration with their colleagues, teachers can, as in the circle meetings just described, do what they can to underline that everybody can learn from everybody else in an enjoyable way.

Richard Wilkinson and Kate Pickett, authors of *The Spirit Level*, have written about what they call 'the poison of inequality', which 'makes some people look as if they are worth much more than others' (Wilkinson and Pickett 2012). In the wider society this is fanned, they claim, by the great inequalities of income and wealth in Britain and similar countries. They write of people's sensitivities to 'being thought less of, disrespected, put down'. Children at school can be brought up in an ethos built around opposite attitudes, where pecking orders of esteem are deliberately challenged. In this way, ideally, no learner will be held back by thoughts of their own inability and low self-worth.

There is much more that could be said about how schools can embody the aims of an aims-based curriculum in their everyday practices, and we have done no more than provide an indication of this. So far, we have put the weight on collective experiences, but there is more to be said, too, about opportunities for individuals to follow up interests of their own, which might or might not involve working with others. This brings us back to the aims-based scheme's stress both on enjoyment and on preparation for autonomous living.

The latter can be a feature of collective learning itself. In a project like the Year 7 exploration of 'Going Places' described above, some learners can spend more time on building siege engines, others on types of world music. Schools can also build in optional activities on the taster/option model suggested on page 18. With the will, and with more resources, we could think even more ambitiously.

One of the more attractive features of education in the former Soviet Union, detachable from the better-known inadequacies of that regime, was its network of 'pioneer houses' and, in the bigger cities, 'pioneer palaces'. Here, after a morning of compulsory lessons, children from different local schools gathered together to pursue activities of their choice. These ranged from looking after animals to assembling radios, learning a foreign language, playing an instrument, and engaging in various sports.

In the Soviet context, all this was laced with indoctrinatory practices to do with being a good Young Pioneer and future member of the Komsomol (League of Young Communists). But it would not be difficult to remodel the idea to suit the very different values of liberal democracy. A young people's centre in every town or suburb, serving all schools in a locality on a mutually convenient timetable, could provide resources that individual schools could not afford. At its senior end, it could be a magnet for older teenagers unattracted by dull local youth clubs and drawn more to the allure of street life.

Here we leave this picture of how an aims-based approach can be applied in practice. It is only, of course, a snapshot.

Assessment

Assessment of students' attainments can serve a number of functions, but is used principally for reasons of accountability and in order to help students in their learning.

On the first of these, citizens have to be assured that schools are doing a good job, and part of this depends on evidence that their students are progressing satisfactorily. This does not entail that the attainments of *every* learner be recorded, still less that they be measured by test or examination results, or that statistics on these be published in league tables. If our aim really is to see how well a school is doing, some more overarching way of finding this out may well be enough.[6]

This will be partly based on how well students are faring, not necessarily each one of them. Given the focus on depth of involvement in learning in the aims-based approach, perhaps the best way of assessing this is by seeing how far students remain committed, once they have finished a course, or finished school, to the activities in which they have been earlier engaged. As things are now, a student can perform well in his or her English Literature exam at 16, but vow never to tangle again with Jane Austen or Shakespeare. If love of the subject, rather than hoop-jumping, is what we want to assess, there is surely a better way.

Another form of assessment is records of student progress (or achievement or attainment). Versions of these can be used in the service of school accountability, and also when students apply for further courses or for employment. They can also be valuable as an aid to learning, not least in an aims-based system. Assessing progress can itself be one of the collaborative activities prominent in the latter. At Wroxham School, for instance, from age 6 upwards children themselves participate with teachers and parents in constructing accounts of how they are getting on. The comments, including comments on comments, are stored electronically and provide valuable material for the children's present teachers and assistants, as well as for staff teaching them in the following year. This kind of assessment system is thus at the same time a learning vehicle for realizing important aims: not only working with others, but, linked with this, self-understanding and appropriate self-regard, respecting others on an equal footing, the virtues of discussion, wholeheartedness of involvement, and the desire to learn more.

Records of progress can be used outside an aims-based system, but they are particularly appropriate to the latter because of the prominence among the more general aims of personal qualities, as well as various kinds of understanding. While conventional examinations can test straightforwardly markable knowledge, they are less well adapted, outside the exact sciences, to assess understanding in depth and the ability to make connections. When it comes to personal qualities, these are beyond their remit altogether.

We see every reason for putting more weight on student records and less on conventional examinations – even in the upper reaches of the secondary school. At present, public examinations dominate the curriculum after age 14. This can lead to a massive restriction, and often perversion, of aims. Passing or doing well in exams at 16 and 18 takes precedence. Many of the aims in our aims-based system are sidelined. Wholehearted engagement in one's science or language studies too often takes a back seat.

As we argued earlier in connection with personal qualities (see page 25):

> ... sensible smaller-scale management of our lives is vital to our well-being. As we grow, we need to develop practical rationality. This is many-sided. It involves some clarity about our goals – not life-goals necessarily, but those found in shorter-term and everyday projects. It requires flexibility in adapting means to ends in pursuit of our goals, as well as sensitivity to which means are acceptable from a moral point of view.

This instrumental virtue of adapting means to ends is vital to a flourishing human life. It finds its place within a larger structure of values within the aims-based scheme. But our present regime narrows its focus. After 14, means–ends planning is largely directed to exam success and all that this connotes: passage to higher studies, to a good job, to a better quality of life. It need not (but well might) encourage attitudes and behaviours that are at odds with the aims we have been advocating, such as:

- not caring about presenting a false picture of oneself to the world via one's question-spottings and other exam techniques, as someone who knows more than he or she does
- aiming directly at increasing one's own well-being – a goal that one may or may not achieve (see page 8) – with too little opportunity to throw oneself into the worthwhile pursuits that *in fact* promote it
- working solely as an individual, rather than often as a cooperating member of a group
- being reinforced in conventional inclinations to rate oneself and others in terms of status rather than as persons worthy of equal respect, exam-passing generally being seen as raising one's status vis-à-vis others; though in some circumstances the opposite occurs, so that students need to hide or even diminish their capabilities
- being likely to apply one's honed skills of blinkered means–ends thinking to other areas of life at the expense of wider ethical considerations.

The defects of our exam-driven 14–19 school system are well known. They are so blatant that one would have expected far more attention to the development and trialling of possible alternatives. In 2004, the Tomlinson Report on 14–19 reform suggested a radical overhaul, with the replacement of GCSEs and A levels by a single diploma, to be taken at various levels (Department for Education 2004). This was to cover not only examination modules, but also an extended essay and a record of wider activities, including work experience, voluntary work, and family responsibilities. If Tomlinson had been implemented, it would have been a step in the direction we have been advocating. But the Labour Government largely rejected it in 2005, many feeling that a great opportunity had been missed.

The Coalition Government has moved in the opposite direction, announcing in September 2012 the replacement of the GCSE by the more restrictive English Baccalaureate (EBacc). This requires high exam marks in English, maths, science, a modern foreign language, and either history or geography. This clutch of exam subjects may well have deep roots in English educational history (it goes back to 1858), but no good justification has been given for it. It would be good to see this backward-looking measure replaced by something more on the lines of Tomlinson, appropriate for all students.

Much of the pressure on school assessment comes from universities and colleges selecting students for courses beginning at 18 or 19. This chronological age has a pivotal role in our thinking about education, both secondary and higher. Everything comes to a head then. It is at that point that the 40–50 per cent of young people who will be going to universities know that their prospects in life are now good, while those who are disappointed look for salvation elsewhere. It is because of such life-determining consequences at 18 or 19 that secondary schools understandably do all they can to prepare their students for examination success. Pressure on students to get the highest possible grades is, unavoidably, intense, with all the pain, anxiety, and fear of failure that this creates.

But despite its ancient pedigree, there is nothing sacrosanct about the practice of going straight on from school to university (a gap year aside) in one's late teens. For the tiny percentage who did so a hundred or more years ago, there was scarcely any alternative. In an age of low life-expectancy, if they wanted – for whatever reason – to deepen and extend their studies beyond school, it was then or never. Nowadays, with many of us living until our eighties and nineties, there should be far less pressure. If we want to go on learning, we have decades more in which to do so. Indeed, the proportion of those who go to UK universities as mature students has been growing for some time.[7]

It is precisely this desire that our aims-based system engenders. The typical late teenager under our scheme will leave school eager to throw himself or herself into further self-chosen absorbing activities of all sorts. Not everyone will want, at that point, to devote most of their time to deeper specialization.

If we could reconceptualize undergraduate study so that it was no longer the norm for it to take place full-time between 18 and 22, this would loosen the stranglehold of public examinations on the school. We can imagine post-school education no longer divided between higher-status institutions called 'universities' (with further pecking orders among them) and further education colleges. There would simply be an ample number of institutions providing a range of courses, part-time and full-time, up to first degree level. Those who might otherwise have gone to university at 18 or 19 would be enabled instead to take up such courses in their mid-twenties or later. These would mainly be for part-time study, with further incentives for full-time sabbaticals. The institutions would also run recreational and retraining courses for much older people, again with some financial support where necessary.

Of course, not *all* young people will wish to defer higher education beyond 18 and those who prefer to go up straight from school will be able to do so, with incentives to do so in shortage subjects, and steps taken to prevent this route becoming (or, rather, remaining) the preserve of those from a more affluent background.

We have spent much of this section on post-school arrangements, but we make no apology for this. If we are to prevent secondary education from being distorted, even perverted, by examination pressures, reform can only come about if we adopt a wider perspective.

School inspection and teacher education

Citizens need to know that their schools are doing a good job. Traditionally in England, this has been principally the function of the inspectorate; in the last 20 years, its work has been supplemented by league tables of test and examination results; and in the last decade or so, the internet has provided more evidence from the schools themselves.

School websites can give remarkably detailed pictures of the institution, including accounts of its aims, highlights of class and school activities, blogs by staff and students, photos, videos, month-by-month archival material, inspection reports, and so on. Not all schools have yet exploited all the possibilities that the internet gives them, but the more imaginative websites show what can be done.[8] And all this in the first few years of web use! How much richer pictures of school life can we expect in the decades to come?

All this, of course, is from the schools' point of view. Citizens need assurance that their self-presentation is accurate, and does not hide unwelcome facts. A general expectation that schools will include on their website data on such things as staff turnover and student attendance may be one kind of corrective. Inspectors will still visit schools, especially where there is cause for concern, and there is every reason why their role should not only be to check up on things, but also, as used to be the case, to advise and to pass on good practice.

As we move towards aims-based learning, we can expect the former role (checking up on things) to change its focus. The inspectors' first task will be to see what policies a school is adopting to implement national aims. They will scrutinize the steps taken to ensure that all teaching staff understand, and are committed to, the scheme as a whole, as expressed in its more general aims. They will see what steps they take, in the light of this understanding and commitment, to translate these aims into student activities and whole-school policies. Of course, they will also want to see whether more determinate aims are being achieved, but never as isolated targets, always in relation to wider canvases.

Teacher education will also shift in its priorities. As of now, in 2013, pre-service work, especially in the various graduate routes (including the one-year Postgraduate Certificate of Education (PGCE), Teach First, and employment-based initial teacher training), has very little room for broad reflection on education and its aims, being more preoccupied with practical competence in the classroom, not least within specific subject areas. No one would want a return of the excessively theory-laden, pre-service courses of the 1960s and 1970s; at this stage, the weight should be firmly on classroom competence. But in an aims-based system, the specifics of classroom life only make sense as implementations of a wider vision. Incoming teachers need to understand the framework within which they will be working. In terms of time allocation, we would need to find a middle road between the theory-rich courses that once obtained and their theory-denuded successors.

Philosophical perspectives, especially in the domains of human nature, ethics, and citizenship, are essential for grasping the content of the kind of aims-based scheme that we have suggested, as well as, even more importantly, the spirit behind it. Forty years ago, when philosophy of education was a dominant component of the PGCE and other such courses, it tended towards the study of semi-discrete topics like the essence of education, issues of equality, punishment, indoctrination, authority, knowledge in the curriculum, and creativity. In an aims-based regime, its offering will be more coherent, with the clear and definite purpose of helping student-teachers to understand and critically reflect on the aims-structure within which they will have to work. Among the related areas into which student-teachers will be inducted are:

- the nature of personal well-being and its constituents
- the role of personal autonomy in a flourishing life and its significance in a liberal democratic polity
- morality and its relationship to personal well-being
- the place of ethical dispositions in personal, moral and civic life, and the kinds of understanding that they involve
- the social nature of human nature.

None of this is to underestimate the place of other 'theoretical' perspectives in pre-service education. An understanding of children, as individuals and as group members, so vital to teaching competence, will continue to rely on the insights of psychology, of both the academic and common-sense varieties. Students will still need to know a lot about the social background, both local and national, of their work (including myths about ability, social class, immigration, and other matters), and about relevant features of the history of their profession.

All this may seem a tall order in a short, one-year course like the PGCE. Indeed it is. With more demanded of our new teachers in the shape of background understanding, there is a strong case, in principle, for extending the PGCE to two years. If we would never dream of allowing a medical doctor to practise after only one year of postgraduate training, whyever should we confine ourselves to this for a teacher?

However, we are well aware that both economic and political forces mean that calls for longer pre-service teacher education have repeatedly fallen on deaf ears. A different approach is to see initial teacher education, of whatever duration, as only one stage in the lifelong learning that enables one to teach well. Even with a lengthier pre-service course, aims-based schooling will require more demanding policies in continuing professional development (CPD). Once qualified, teachers will begin to be policy-makers, helping their school to find useful and imaginative ways of giving concrete form to national aims. This means development on two fronts: a deepening understanding of the aims; and creativity in implementing them. Both aspects bring with them collaboration with other staff, students, parents, and others.

A good school will see the in-service education of its staff as one of its highest priorities,[9] to be undertaken largely in and by the school itself, with encouragement to study good practice elsewhere and to take CPD courses in universities where appropriate.

Facing political realities

The previous section spelt out how an aims-based curriculum could be put into practice. It described a recommended division in responsibilities between the political and professional realms, looked at the range of schools (including private schools) it should cover, suggested how it might operate within a school, and examined implications for assessment, inspection, and teacher education.

But this is unlikely to satisfy the policy-maker, say a minister or shadow minister interested in the broad concept of an aims-based curriculum and looking for guidance on how to introduce it. For the previous section remains at an ideal level: it shows how an aims-based curriculum might look in practice, but does little or nothing to indicate how we may go forward *from where we are*. Education ministers or would-be ministers understandably grow impatient with longer-term visions untethered to present realities. They want to know what steps we can take *now*.

Let us see what headway we can make on this. We have at present a subject-based, rather than an aims-based, curriculum. The first cannot change into the second overnight. The best we can hope for is a more gradual shift towards it.

There have been recent examples of aims-based schemes that meet the subject-based approach halfway. The first, and still the most ambitious, has been Northern Ireland's 'Pathways' programme for Key Stage 3 (age 11–14), introduced in 2003 by the Council for the Curriculum, Examinations and Assessment (CCEA). This was built around an organized array of aims to do with students as individuals, as contributors to society, and as contributors to the economy and environment. It was obliged to retain a traditional subject structure, but employed various devices to help subjects reconceptualize themselves as vehicles of the aims and to reduce their inward-facing predilections – for instance, grouping them together in 'general learning areas'; bringing their internal aims into line with overall aims; and encouraging collaboration between subjects and integrated projects.

In 2004, the Scottish Government published *A Curriculum for Excellence* (Curriculum Review Group 2004). This was also centred around a set of overall aims to be mapped onto familiar curriculum content. The national aims are fourfold: they seek to enable all young people to become successful learners, confident individuals, responsible citizens, and effective contributors. Under each heading is a list of more specific aims.

In 2007, England adopted a very similar list of aims for its new Key Stage 3 and Key Stage 4 curriculum (Department for Children, Schools and Families 2007). They were meant to bear on the rest of the curriculum, by standing at the head of programmes of study in different subjects, and by helping to shape the subjects' self-descriptions under the rubric of '*The importance of* ... [history, science, etc.]' (Department for Education 2012).

A fatal weakness of the English reform, echoed elsewhere, is that existing school subjects remain sacrosanct. This is not an aims-based curriculum, but still a subject-based one, now with aims added *post hoc.* Subjects have their own aims, often directed understandably towards induction into their specialism. With decades, if not centuries, of programme-honing behind them, they are more likely to keep close to their old ways than to give their curricula the radical shake-up they would need to conform to the more global aims.

Since the Coalition came to power in 2010, the grip of traditional subjects like English, mathematics, science, history, geography, and modern foreign languages has grown ever stronger, both in primary schools and in secondaries. In the latter, this has been despite the exodus of nearly half the schools from National Curriculum control as they have converted to academies. Curriculum control is now to be exercised partly by the new 'English Baccalaureate' (EBacc), an award at age 16 for high performance in the GCSE, in five subjects: English, mathematics, science, a modern foreign language, and either history or geography (see above page 58).

In addition, since 2010 ministers have been more ready to intervene in curricular details normally left to professional discretion. The most notable example is in their insistence on synthetic phonics as the way to teach reading in primary schools.

This, then, is where we are now – in a period of reinforced subject-centredness, with fading memories of a somewhat timid attempt to move towards something more aims-centred. How might we move forward at national policy-making level?

Twenty practical suggestions

Here is a list of 20 practical suggestions, many of which summarize arguments that we have presented above. These suggestions are not necessarily meant to be introduced in the order presented below.

1. Establish a national commission, protected from political meddling, to act as trustee for a defensible national curriculum. Its task should be to work out a unified set of aims befitting our liberal democracy, stretching from general to specific.

2. Go back to the 2007 reforms in England and those that preceded them in Scotland and Northern Ireland. This means dismantling Coalition moves towards subject-centredness, including the EBacc, at least in its present form, and also ministerial meddling in classroom specifics, as in the teaching of reading. It also means constructing and setting out a number of defensible overall aims, not simply as a list (as in 2007), but with a rationale attached.

3. As in 2007 in England, take steps to bring existing subjects into line with the aims. Ask each subject association, together with partner professional organizations, to review the subject's curriculum content in the light of the aims, cutting out and adding where appropriate, and being able publicly to justify such judgements.

4. Encourage schools, both primary and secondary, to find ways of making subject offerings less discrete through interdisciplinary cooperation, themes, projects, etc., that promote the aims. One possible route is the creation of 'learning areas' between the aims and the subjects, as in the CCEA 'Pathways' programme. More flexible, and more suited to the digital age to which we have grown used since the CCEA reforms, is a centre-led initiative to link schools together on the internet, as well as by face-to-face contact, so that good practice in breaking down subject barriers can be spread across the system. The 2007 reforms were accompanied by an interactive website for cross-curricular school planning. This has been removed by the Coalition Government, but should be reinstated (Association of School and College Leaders 2011).

5. Work towards a general agreement between government and subject associations to put general aims above sectional interests and to promote interdisciplinary cooperation.

6. Make planning more flexible, and diminish overcrowding in the curriculum, by rethinking the practice of giving a subject protected status on the curriculum for a set number of years (e.g. mathematics for 11 years, history for 9 years). Put the focus less on how long a student should be studying subject X and more on what aspects of X are necessary to meet overall aims.

7. Extend the National Curriculum to age 18 with the raising of school-leaving age.

8. Make the National Curriculum a matter of non-statutory guidance (as in Scotland), rather than mandatory.

9. Extend the National Curriculum to all schools, including private ones.

10. In time, when some of these other suggested reforms are in place, remove mention of discrete subjects from the National Curriculum, thus making the latter wholly a set of national aims, including sub-aims that draw on scientific, historical, practical, literary material, etc.

11. Emphasize schools' right and responsibility to meet these national aims in ways they find most appropriate, whether by discrete subject teaching or in other ways.

12. Establish national expectations in progress towards fulfilling national aims at age 11. Take steps to encourage collaboration on meeting these expectations at age 11 among primary and secondary schools in each local area.

13. In the interests of accountability, ensure that each school maintains a full and constantly updated website, showing how it is trying to realize national aims. Specific criteria may need to be satisfied here.

14. Reorientate Ofsted, so as to make the inspectors' central task to see what policies a school is adopting to implement national aims, and scrutinize the steps taken to ensure that all teaching staff understand and are committed to the scheme as a whole, and take steps to translate these aims into student activities and whole-school policies. Redirect Ofsted towards a supportive rather than grading role, so that it can help schools to take aims seriously.

15. Highlight in pre-service teacher education and CPD the importance of aims, their rationale and flexibility in choice of means, focusing on interdisciplinary projects as well as work within subjects.

16. Encourage schools to use jointly agreed records of achievement (e.g. as e-portfolios) as a way of recording individual teachers' CPD in this and other areas. These can form part of higher degree work in education, as well as being used in promotion procedures.

17. Abolish the few remaining SATs and enable all schools to use cumulative records of achievement covering the whole spectrum of national aims and involving students and their parents/guardians in constructing these records.

18. Provide incentives for all school leavers to continue part-time study (with opportunities for some full-time study) at a local college, e.g. free tuition, perhaps using a voucher system, up to a certain level (e.g. part-way through an undergraduate course), with student loans beyond that. Make these arrangements available to those who do not want to move into post-school education at 18 but when they are older.

19. Encourage the growth of a network of local institutions offering part-time, post-school education up to graduate level. These institutions would cover work now done in universities and FE colleges, thus further eroding the artificial distinction between these two sectors. These institutions would encourage students to move upwards or sideways on a 'learning without limits' principle.

20. Oblige these local institutions to take all-comers, using school records of achievement to guide new students into courses at the most appropriate level. Reduce in this way the incentive for school students to take conventional exams at 16 and 18, thus freeing schools from the stranglehold of excessive examination requirements at 14–19.

Conclusion

Everyone will agree that schools need aims. But too often the ones suggested are confined to very general statements about desirable outcomes and not followed through into anything more determinate.

Curriculum planners across the world, from those in government to those in schools, often leave these aims as high-level mission statements and, when it comes to mapping out curriculum activities, look elsewhere. The framework they use, earliest years apart, tends to be based around separate subjects. The coherence of students' education is thereby imperilled. Like the curriculum planners, they soon begin to think of their school experience as parcelled into discrete boxes.

This book has argued for something more holistic – an aims-based curriculum, or ABC. It has rejected the view that aims cannot but float over the school curriculum in some cloud-land of their own. They can and should inform school learning at every point.

The way forward is to start with a defensible set of general aims appropriate to the liberal democracy in which we aspire to live, to clarify what these involve so as to reduce the likelihood of radically divergent interpretations, and to derive lower-level aims from these in the iterative process that we have outlined in the body of this book. At the end of this process, we reach aims at least as specific as any curriculum items found in current regimes. Many of them will indeed be very close to such items, or at least will seem to be. The crucial difference, however, is that these very specific ABC aims will constantly be reminding learners, teachers, and planners alike that larger, global aims lie behind them, which lead back to central questions about what education should be for.

As we have said more than once, at this more specific level we have not sought to produce a definitive list of items. This is partly because, owing to the breadth of a student's learning experience, we have not been able to go into detail in every area, but have merely given one or two illustrations. But, in any case, there is no sharp line between what mature persons may be expected to be, understand, know how to do, etc., and what schools should contribute to this. Since the work that schools can do is bound to be incomplete, they should be aiming at setting their students firmly on a path ahead, rather than targeting comprehensiveness of coverage.

Since schools tend to work within subject-blocks, the spotlight tends to fall on the items of *knowledge* that these demand – not least for success in public examinations. In the new scheme, the acquisition of knowledge – both knowledge of truths about the world and knowledge of how to do things (e.g. read, write, add up, navigate the internet) – is more clearly subordinated to *personal qualities*. The sort of person the student is becoming is the chief consideration. This necessitates knowing a lot of things, but possessing this knowledge is not the main aim.

In our present system, knowledge possession may not be quite as central as it looks. For what schools may be doing, with their more successful students, is helping to shape the sort of person who is good at assimilating and using knowledge, who grows in confidence with success, who perhaps sees himself or herself as a cut above other people and on track towards an elite job and lifestyle. Other students, on the other hand, may come to see academic learning as not for them, to expect to fail, to view themselves as the kind of person who can only flourish, if at all, outside school.

Far better than keeping attitudes and habits in the shadows is to place them under the spotlight. Schools' main job should be to nurture *desirable dispositions in every learner*. That is why so much of this book has been taken up with describing these dispositions and showing their overall rationale.

The road to an ABC will not be built in a day, or even a decade. Conventional, subject-based ways of organizing school curricula have a long pedigree, which can indeed be traced back to the sixteenth century (White 2011b). Over this time, in Western countries, they have won out over the rival, classics-based, notion of elite schooling. In the last two hundred years in most Western countries and in the last hundred more globally, boxed sets of subjects have made up the main curriculum package, at first for aspiring social classes and later for whole populations. Challenging this tradition will not be easy. It is deeply entrenched in every aspect of school education, not only in timetabling arrangements, but also in assessment, inspection, teacher education and, to a certain extent, teacher identity. Subject associations are powerful pressure groups that protect the integrity of their discipline and are chary of moving too far from the status quo. Parents, all of whom, like every other citizen, have been through the school system, are inclined to see education in conventional, subject-structured terms. Parents and other citizens are also voters. Even progressive governments will think twice before departing too far or too rapidly from the familiar pattern.

Yet this is the only sensible way forward. The educational system has a life of its own. It sees itself as at the service of the learner, and much of its work is indeed so directed. At the same time, it is deeply attached to its own *modi operandi*, and where there are conflicts between these and promoting the personal and civic well-being of the student, the former can occasionally take precedence. Schools can, and sometimes do, stream students, select or exclude them, indoctrinate them in a belief system, compel them to attend classes in this subject or that, regulate their clothing, require them to ask for permission to use the toilet, look askance at their challenges to authority, oblige them to face the rigours and anxieties of exam preparation, drill them in exam techniques … We are not saying that such things are never in the students' interests, only that these can sometimes get sidelined.

The next big step for educational reform is to ensure that the learner's well-being, broadly conceived,[10] is always at the centre of the school's concern. The key to this is reconceptualizing how we see the school curriculum. This means putting the curriculum on a less tradition-bound foundation. It means making sure that it is well grounded at every point in a set of aims fit for a twenty-first century liberal democracy.

Notes

[1] We are not, of course, against subjects per se. Our point is that they should not be the starting point for a school's curriculum. See Young, M.F.D. (2010) 'The future of education in a knowledge society: The radical case for a subject-based curriculum'. *Journal of the Pacific Circle Consortium for Education*, 22, 21–32.

[2] For example Ziman, J. (2000) *Real Science: What it is, and what it means* (Cambridge: Cambridge University Press).

[3] For further considerations about the nature of well-being, see Cigman, R. (2012) 'We need to talk about well-being'. *Research Papers in Education*, 27 (4), 449–62, online at www.tandfonline.com/doi/abs/10.1080/02671522.2012.690238 (accessed 22 November 2012).

[4] We have in mind only schools offering a programme of general education.

[5] For a book-length account of Wroxham School, see Swann, M. *et al.* (2012) *Creating Learning without Limits* (Maidenhead: Open University Press).

[6] A model exists in the work of the Assessment of Performance Unit that operated in the UK outside Scotland in the 1970s and 1980s. This conducted tests in different subjects at 11 and 15 for *samples* of students, with the aim of monitoring attainments, and changes in attainments, at national level.

[7] UCAS (2012) *Mature Students' Guide* (Cheltenham: UCAS), online at www.ucas.com/documents/ucasguides/maturestudentsguide2013.pdf (accessed 30 September 2012).

[8] See, for instance, www.thewroxham.net

[9] See, for instance, Swann, M. *et al.* (2012) *Creating Learning without Limits* (Maidenhead: Open University Press).

[10] That is, to include his or her moral and civic engagement.

References

Association of School and College Leaders (2011) 'Response to the Labour Party Curriculum Policy Review'. Online. www.ascl.org.uk/opinion/consultation_responses/labour_party_curriculum_policy_review (accessed 15 August 2012).

Bassey, M. (2011) *Education for the Inevitable: Schooling when the oil runs out*. Brighton: Book Guild.

Beck, J. (1998) *Morality and Citizenship in Education*. London: Cassell.

Boaler, J. (2009) *The Elephant in the Classroom: Helping children learn and love maths*. London: Souvenir Press.

Bramall, S. and White, J. (eds) (2000) *Why Learn Maths?* London: Institute of Education, University of London.

Bruner, J. (1960) *The Process of Education*. New York: Random House.

Cannadine, D., Keating, J. and Sheldon, N. (2011) *The Right Kind of History: Teaching the past in twentieth-century England*. Basingstoke: Palgrave Macmillan.

Cigman, R. (2012) 'We need to talk about well-being'. *Research Papers in Education*, 27 (4), 449–62. Online. www.tandfonline.com/doi/abs/10.1080/02671522.2012.690238 (accessed 22 November 2012).

Collins, H. and Evans, R. (2007) *Rethinking Expertise*. Chicago: University of Chicago Press.

Curriculum Review Group (2004) *A Curriculum for Excellence*. Edinburgh: Scottish Executive. Online. www.scotland.gov.uk/Resource/Doc/26800/0023690.pdf (accessed 6 October 2012).

Department for Children, Schools and Families/Qualifications and Curriculum Authority (2007) *The National Curriculum Statutory Requirements for Key Stages 3 and 4*. London: DCSF and QCA.

Department for Education (2004) *Final Report of the Working Group on 14–19 Reform*. London: DfE.

Department for Education (2011) *The Framework for the National Curriculum: A report by the Expert Panel for the National Curriculum review*. Online. www.education.gov.uk/publications/standard/publicationDetail/Page1/DFE-00135-2011 (accessed 15 January 2012).

Department for Education (2012) *Secondary Curriculum Subjects*. Online. www.education.gov.uk/schools/teachingandlearning/curriculum/secondary (accessed 30 September 2012).

European Commission (2004) *Europe Needs More Scientists: Report by the High Level Group on Increasing Human Resources for Science and Technology*. Brussels: European Commission.

Every Child a Chance Trust (2009) *The Long Term Costs of Numeracy Difficulties*. Online. www.nationalnumeracy.org.uk/resources/14/index.html (accessed 18 January 2013).

Giddens, A. (1991) *Modernity and Self-identity: Self and society in the late modern age*. Cambridge: Polity Press.

Hacker, A. (2012) 'Is algebra necessary?' *New York Times Sunday Review*, 29 July, SR1. Online. www.nytimes.com/2012/07/29/opinion/sunday/is-algebra-necessary.html? (accessed 31 July 2012).

Halstead, J.M. and Reiss, M.J. (2003) *Values in Sex Education: From principles to practice*. London: RoutledgeFalmer.

Hand, M. (2011) *Patriotism in Schools*, Philosophy of Education Society of Great Britain. Online. http://onlinelibrary.wiley.com/doi/10.1111/j.2048-416X.2011.00001.x/pdf (accessed 30 September 2012).

Harlen, W. (2010) (ed.) *Principles and Big Ideas of Science Education.* Association for Science Education. Online. www.ase.org.uk/documents/principles-and-big-ideas-of-science-education (accessed 30 September 2012).

Hawkins, E. (2005) 'Out of this nettle, drop-out, we pluck this flower, opportunity: Re-thinking the school foreign language apprenticeship', *Language Learning Journal*, 32, 4–17.

Hodgen, J. and Pepper, D. (2010) *Is the UK an Outlier? An international comparison of upper secondary mathematics education.* London: Nuffield Foundation.

Lambert, D. and Morgan, J. (2010) *Teaching Geography 11–18: A conceptual approach.* Maidenhead: Open University Press.

Morgan, C., Watson, A. and Tikly, C. (2004) *Teaching School Subjects 11–19: Mathematics.* London: RoutledgeFalmer.

National Academy of Sciences Committee on Science Engineering and Public Policy (2007) *Rising Above the Gathering Storm: Energizing and employing America for a brighter economic future.* Washington DC: National Academies Press.

New Visions for Education Group (2010) 'The Curriculum' (*Much improved: Should do even better* March 2010 e-paper 10). Online. www.newvisionsforeducation.org.uk/wp-content/uploads/2010/12/10-The-Curriculum.pdf (accessed 26 November 2012).

Raz, J. (1994) 'Multiculturalism: A liberal perspective'. In Raz, J. (ed.), *Ethics in the Public Domain.* Oxford: Clarendon Press, 155–76.

Royal Society (2012) *Shut Down or Restart? The way forward for computing in UK schools.* London: Royal Society. Online. http://royalsociety.org/uploadedFiles/Royal_Society_Content/education/policy/computing-in-schools/2012-01-12-Computing-in-Schools.pdf (accessed 30 September 2012).

St John's, Marlborough (n.d.) *Why Do We Need an Alternative Curriculum?* Online. www.stjohns.wilts.sch.uk/resources/curriculum/StJAlternativeCurriculum.pdf (accessed 5 October 2012).

Swann, M., Peacock, A., Hart, S. and Drummond, M.J. (2012) *Creating Learning without Limits.* Maidenhead: Open University Press.

UCAS (2012) *Mature Students' Guide.* Cheltenham: UCAS. Online. www.ucas.com/documents/ucasguides/maturestudentsguide2013.pdf (accessed 30 September 2012).

White, J. (2011a) *Exploring Well-Being in Schools: A guide to making children's lives more fulfilling.* London: Routledge.

White, J. (2011b) *The Invention of the Secondary Curriculum.* New York: Palgrave Macmillan.

White, J. (2012) 'Philosophy in primary schools?'. *Journal of Philosophy of Education*, 46, 449–60.

White, P. (1994) 'Parental choice and education for citizenship'. In Halstead, M. (ed.), *Parental Choice and Education: Principles, policies and practice.* London: Kogan Page.

Wilkinson, R. and Pickett, K. (2012) 'The poison of inequality was behind last summer's riots', *The Guardian*, 5 August.

Williams, K. (2000) *Why Teach Foreign Languages in Schools? A philosophical response to curriculum policy.* Special issue of *Impact*, 5, vii–46. Online. http://onlinelibrary.wiley.com/doi/10.1111/j.2048-416X.2000.tb00032.x/pdf

Wilson, J. (1990) *A New Introduction to Moral Education.* London: Cassell.

Young, M.F.D. (2010) 'The future of education in a knowledge society: The radical case for a subject-based curriculum'. *Journal of the Pacific Circle Consortium for Education*, 22, 21–32.

Ziman, J. (2000) *Real Science: What it is, and what it means.* Cambridge: Cambridge University Press.

Index